Moh

Non-Functional Requirements

Mohamad Kassab

Non-Functional Requirements

Modeling and Assessment

VDM Verlag Dr. Müller

Impressum/Imprint (nur für Deutschland/ only for Germany)

Bibliografische Information der Deutschen Nationalbibliothek: Die Deutsche Nationalbibliothek verzeichnet diese Publikation in der Deutschen Nationalbibliografie; detaillierte bibliografische Daten sind im Internet über http://dnb.d-nb.de abrufbar.
Alle in diesem Buch genannten Marken und Produktnamen unterliegen warenzeichen-, marken- oder patentrechtlichem Schutz bzw. sind Warenzeichen oder eingetragene Warenzeichen der jeweiligen Inhaber. Die Wiedergabe von Marken, Produktnamen, Gebrauchsnamen, Handelsnamen, Warenbezeichnungen u.s.w. in diesem Werk berechtigt auch ohne besondere Kennzeichnung nicht zu der Annahme, dass solche Namen im Sinne der Warenzeichen- und Markenschutzgesetzgebung als frei zu betrachten wären und daher von jedermann benutzt werden dürften.

Coverbild: www.purestockx.com

Verlag: VDM Verlag Dr. Müller Aktiengesellschaft & Co. KG
Dudweiler Landstr. 99, 66123 Saarbrücken, Deutschland
Telefon +49 681 9100-698, Telefax +49 681 9100-988, Email: info@vdm-verlag.de
Zugl.: Montreal, Concordia University, Diss., 2009

Herstellung in Deutschland:
Schaltungsdienst Lange o.H.G., Berlin
Books on Demand GmbH, Norderstedt
Reha GmbH, Saarbrücken
Amazon Distribution GmbH, Leipzig
ISBN: 978-3-639-20617-3

Imprint (only for USA, GB)

Bibliographic information published by the Deutsche Nationalbibliothek: The Deutsche Nationalbibliothek lists this publication in the Deutsche Nationalbibliografie; detailed bibliographic data are available in the Internet at http://dnb.d-nb.de .
Any brand names and product names mentioned in this book are subject to trademark, brand or patent protection and are trademarks or registered trademarks of their respective holders. The use of brand names, product names, common names, trade names, product descriptions etc. even without a particular marking in this works is in no way to be construed to mean that such names may be regarded as unrestricted in respect of trademark and brand protection legislation and could thus be used by anyone.

Cover image: www.purestockx.com

Publisher:
VDM Verlag Dr. Müller Aktiengesellschaft & Co. KG
Dudweiler Landstr. 99, 66123 Saarbrücken, Germany
Phone +49 681 9100-698, Fax +49 681 9100-988, Email: info@vdm-publishing.com

Printed in the U.S.A.
Printed in the U.K. by (see last page)
ISBN: 978-3-639-20617-3

Table of Contents

To My Family…

Chapter I: Introduction

"When I'm working on a problem, I never think about beauty. I think only how to solve the problem. But when I have finished, if the solution is not beautiful, I know it is wrong."
R. Buckminster Fuller (1895 – 1983).

1.1 Motivation

In the early phases of software development, user requirements are established based on an analysis of business goals and of the application domain. Subsequently, architectures of the desired systems are designed and implemented. During this development process, requirements are usually exposed to many changes, as the availability of knowledge on the system under development increases [Jac07].

Software systems are characterized both by their functional behavior (what the system does) and by their nonfunctional behavior (how the system behaves with respect to some observable attributes like reliability, reusability, maintainability, etc.). In the software market place, in which functionally equivalent products compete for the same customer, Non Functional Requirements (NFRs) become more important in distinguishing between the competing products. However, in practice, NFRs receive little attention relative to Functional Requirements (FRs) [WW03]. This is mainly because of the nature of these requirements which poses a challenge when taking the choice of treating them at an early stage of the development process. NFRs are subjective, relative and they tend to become scattered among multiple modules when they are mapped from the requirements domain to the solution space. Furthermore, NFRs can often interact, in the sense that attempts to achieve one NFR can help or hinder the achievement of other NFRs at particular software functionality. Such an interaction creates an extensive network of interdependencies and tradeoffs among NFRs which is not easy to trace or estimate [CNYM00]. Nevertheless, reports consistently indicate that neglecting NFRs can lead to catastrophic project failures, or, at the very least, to considerable delays and consequently to significant increases in the final cost. The following list provides valid examples:

• London Ambulance System (LAS) [FD96]: In 1992, The London Ambulance Service introduced a new computer-aided dispatch system which was intended to automate the system that dispatched ambulances in response to calls from the public and the emergency services. This new system was extremely inefficient and ambulance response times increased markedly. Shortly after its introduction, it failed completely and LAS reverted to the previous manual system. The failure of the system was mainly due to a failure to consider "*human and organizational factors*" in the design of the system.

- Mars Climate Orbiter [BLF99]: This was one of two NASA spacecrafts in the Mars Surveyor '98 program. The mission failed because of software "*interoperability*" issue. The craft drifted off course during its voyage and entered a much lower orbit than planned, and was destroyed by atmospheric friction. The metric/imperial mix-up which destroyed the craft was caused by a software error back on Earth. The thrusters on the spacecraft which were intended to control its rate of rotation were controlled by a computer which underestimated the effect of the thrusters by a factor of 4.45. This is the ratio between a pound force - the standard unit of force in the imperial system - and a Newton, the standard unit in the metric system. The software on Earth was working in pounds force, while the spacecraft expected figures in Newton.

- Therac 25: The Medical Linear accelerator [LT93]: This was a radiation therapy machine. It was involved with at least six accidents between 1985 and 1987, in which patients were given massive overdoses of radiation, approximately 100 times the intended dose. Three of the six patients died as a direct consequence. These accidents highlighted the dangers of software control of "*safety*"-critical systems, and they have become a standard case study in health informatics.

- Siemens: Possible Hearing Damage in Some Cell Phones [SIEMENS04]: In 2004, Siemens issued a "*safety*" warning that some of its cell phones may have a software problem that could cause them to emit a loud noise, possibly causing hearing loss for the phone user. The malfunction happens only if, while the phone is in use, the battery runs down to the point that the phone automatically disconnects the call and begins to shut down.

- The New Jersey Department of Motor Vehicles' licensing system [Bab85]: This system was written in the fourth-generation programming language, ideal to save development time. When implemented, the system was so slow that at one point more than million New Jersey vehicles roamed the streets with unprocessed license renewals. The project aimed at satisfying "*affordability*" and "*timeliness*" objectives, but failed due to "*performance scalability*" problems.

- The initial design of the ARPANet Interface Message Process software [BI96]: This project focused on "performance" at the expense of "*evolvability*" by designing an extremely tight inner loop.

- The National Library of Medicine MEDLARS II system [BI96]: The project was initially developed with many layers of abstraction to support a wide range of future publication systems.

The initial focus of the system was towards improving "portability" and "evolvability" qualities. The system was scrapped after two expensive hardware upgrades due to *"performance"* problems.

Despite this obvious importance and relevance of NFRs, they are almost always left to be verified after the implementation is finished, which means NFRs are not mapped directly and explicitly from requirements engineering to implementation [SURVEY1]. This is mainly due to the enormous pressure towards deploying software as fast as possible. This leaves software development with potential exacerbation of the age-old problem of requirements errors that are not detected until very late in the process. The authors of [NLC00] enumerate some of the well-known problems of the software development due of the NFRs omission: (i) Cost and schedule overruns, (ii) Software systems discontinuation and (iii) Dissatisfaction of software systems users. For all that, it is important to affirm that NFR should affect all levels of software life cycle and shall be identified as soon as possible and their elicitation must be accurate and complete.

1.2 Problem Statement

Once a software system has been deployed, it is typically straightforward to observe whether or not a certain FR has been met, as the areas of success or failure in their context can be rigidly defined. However, the same is not true for NFRs as these can refer to concepts that can be interdependent and difficult to measure.

The problem of lacking any early NFR integration within the specified system is likely to cause an increase in the effort and maintenance overhead [SDM05]. The importance of software compliance with the imposed NFRs requires management of their scope, which brings up the importance of clearly defining, tracing and effort estimating the complex and frequently ill-defined NFRs and their interrelations in increasingly complex large-scale software system.

This book identifies three major areas to investigate:

1- NFRs Conceptualization: In general, and because of their diverse nature, NFRs have been (at best) specified in loose, fuzzy terms that are open to wide ranging and subjective interpretation. As such, they provide little guidance to architects and engineers as they make the already tough trade-offs necessary to meet schedule pressures and functionality goals. For instance, most software engineering approaches [IEEE98], [JBR99], [Gra92] and industrial practices specify NFRs separately from FRs of a system. This is mainly because the early integration of NFRs is difficult to achieve and usually accomplished at the later phases of the software development process. However, since the integration is not supported from the requirements phase to the implementation phase, some of the software engineering principles such as abstraction, localization, modularization, uniformity and reusability, can be compromised. Furthermore, the resulting system is more difficult to maintain and evolve.

Instead, NFRs need to be made precise and clear right from the requirements phase. But in order to be able to specify the NFRs in precise terms, there must be a general understanding to what the term NFR stands for, and what are the relations that the NFR may be exposed to during the lifecycle of the project. In fact, although the term "non-functional requirement" has been in use for more than 20 years, there is still no consensus in the requirements engineering community what NFRs are and what are relations that an individual NFR may participate in.

2- NFRs Traceability: According to recent publications [KIC05], [Dan05], [BKW03] and [FE00] in requirements engineering, there is a multifaceted gap between requirements and the developed solution. Traditional software development approaches do not address this gap. For example, architectural design methods that link architecture to requirements make architecture a central concern. These methods use requirements as input only or as a standard for evaluation [BCK03] and [CKK01] and disregard current requirements engineering processes. Frequently, existing approaches fail to convey change, rationale, options, and organizational implications of requirements or of solution designs [TA05]. The gap between requirements engineering and solution design seems to be essentially a problem of traceability.

Traceability has so far been tackled mainly qualitatively, identifying related elements in requirements engineering and solution to visualize those elements of solution impacted by changing requirements and vice versa.

Tracing NFRs from requirements engineering to solution design poses further challenges as these requirements tend to scatter among multiple modules when they are mapped from the requirements domain to the solution space. Another challenge arises as the existing approaches to model NFRs lack an adequate specification of the semantics of NFRs, which leads to inconsistent interpretational uses of these requirements.

3- Effort Estimation of building NFRs: Estimating the effort is an important task in software project management [EDBS04]. A realistic effort estimation right from the start in a project gives the project manager confidence about any future course of action, since many of the decisions made during development depend on, or are influenced by, the initial effort estimations. NFRs are very challenging when estimating the effort and the time it would take to implement them [CNYM00]. This is mainly because of the unique nature of these requirements: NFRs are subjective, relative, interacting and crosscutting. However, it is crucial to be able to make decisions about the scope of software by given resources and budget based on a proper estimation of building both FRs and NFRs.

1.3 Research Goals

Drawing on the discussion in the previous section, the goal of this research contributes to a formal, integrated and quantitative approach to modeling and assessing NFRs. The research aims at: building a systematic and formal approach to NFRs modeling, tracing, impact detection and effort estimation from the early stages of the software development process. Central to such an approach is the definition of the NFRs Ontology for capturing and structuring the knowledge on the software requirements (FRs and NFRs), their refinements, and their interdependencies. This research contributes towards achieving the overall goal of managing the attainable scope and the changes of NFRs.

The key research questions that will drive us towards achieving the research goals are discussed in the methodology section (Chapter 3, Section 3.2).

1.4 Research Outline

In order to facilitate the introduction of the body of work completed in this work, we have used the Basili et al. framework [BSH86] and [Bas96] to help in outlining the research work process, as well as to provide classification scheme for understanding and evaluating the work. A schematic representation of this framework is presented in Figure 1-1.

I Definition					
Motivation	Object	Purpose	Perspective	Domain	Scope
II Planning					
Design		Criteria		Measurement	
III Operation					
Preparation		Execution		Data Analysis	
IV Interpretation					
Context of Interpretation			Extrapolation		

Figure 1-1: Basili et al. Framework [BSH86]

The framework consists of four categories corresponding to phases of: 1) Definition, 2) Planning, 3) Operation and 4) Interpretation.

During the definition phase, an intuitive understanding of a high-level problem is developed into a precise specification that could contribute to its solution.

The study definition phase contains six parts: 1) Motivation, 2) Object, 3) Purpose, 4) Perspective, 5) Domain and 6) Scope.

The Motivation component identifies the high-level problem to be tackled and it was presented in Section 1.1 of this chapter.

The Object component defines the principal entity being studied which corresponds to the NFR in the software development process.

The Purpose is the explicit problem to be resolved which; as described in Section 1.2 of this chapter, corresponds to (i) *characterize* the concept of NFR and its relations with other concepts in the requirements engineering discipline, (ii) *improve* the NFRs traceability practice and (iii) *predict* the effort of building the software project taking the NFRs into consideration.

The Perspective specifies from what point of view the explicit problem will be addressed. In our study, this corresponds to the researchers in the requirements engineering field and the participators in software industry.

This work represents: (i) an observational study, where there are no controlled variables and (ii) an experimental study [BSH86], [WRHRW00], [JM01] and [Bas96]; where at least one treatment or controlled variable exists.

Usually, an experiment in software engineering has two domains [BSH86] and [Bas96]: Team and project. Teams (comprising one or more members) work on software projects that attempt to resolve an issue, in terms of a software deliverable (manual, program and specifications). A general classification of the scope of experiments can be obtained by examining the sizes of the two domains considered. Four combinations of domains are possible: One team working on one project (single project), many teams working on one project (replicated project), one team working on many projects (multiple-project variation) and a combination of many teams and projects (blocked subject-project).

On the other hand, the observational study has two domains: Number of sites included and whether or not a set of study variables are determined a priori. Whether or not a set of study variables are predetermined by the researcher separates the pure qualitative study, (no a priori variables isolated by the observer), from the mix of qualitative and quantitative analysis, where the observer has identified, a priori, a set of variables for observation. The four possible combinations of the domains which form the possible scope for an observational study are: One site where a priori has been identified (case study), one site where a priori has not been identified (case qualitative study), more than one site where a priori has been identified (field study), more than one site where a priori has not been identified (field qualitative study).

There are several attributes which characterize this work study depending on the identified purpose:

1- Characterizing NFRs: this is an observational study in which the evaluation is performed through field study with both students not experienced in the study of domain (novice) and people with experience in the study of domain (experts). The evaluation has been conducted in the field under normal conditions (vivo).

2- NFRs traceability: This is an observational study which has been discussed through a context of a case study and which has been evaluated by multi-project variation experiment. The evaluation has been conducted with experts from the NOKIA team in Montréal and has been conducted under normal working conditions (vivo).

3- NFRs Effort Estimation: This is an observational study which has been evaluated by case study. The evaluation has been conducted by students which are not experienced in the domain of the research study (novice) and has been run in the field under normal conditions (vivo).

Our research was planned in detail in the second phase of the framework. During the design step, the case studies were selected (see Chapter 3, Section 3.3). The direct and indirect criteria or factors that are related to the research' purpose were identified. Then, the measures designed to quantify these direct and indirect criteria were determined.

The research work itself is actually carried out during the third phase of the framework: Training was given when it is required for the team that will be taking the measurements. Data are collected, analyzed and evaluated during the execution of the case studies. These data are then analyzed using suitable techniques chosen during the design step as would be explained in this book.

1.5 Major Contributions

The major contributions of this book have been published (or accepted for publishing) in the following book [KOD10], journal [SOKH09], conference proceedings and workshops [KOD09b], [KOD09a], [KOD08c], [KOD08b], [KOD08a], [KOD07b], [KOD07a], [KDO07a], [DKPWO07], [KO06], [KDO07b] and [KDO09].

While this research work blends the disciplines of software measurement, requirements engineering, and software architectural design in a cohesive fashion, the novelty of our approach lies in the following aspects:

1- It proposes a formal model for NFRs and their relations. The model is captured through a Common Foundation for NFRs, i.e. the shared meaning of terms and concepts in the domain of NFRs. The Common Foundation will be realized by developing a problem domain ontology for NFRs and related domain knowledge. This NFRs Ontology is adequate for projects taking into consideration the NFRs and their relations earlier in the software development and throughout the life cycle.

2- It provides a mechanism for NFRs conflicts identification based on the constructed ontology.

3- It proposes a change management mechanism for tracing the impact of NFRs on the other constructs in the ontology and vice versa, and provides a traceability mechanism using Datalog expressions to implement queries on the relational model-based representation for the ontology. An alternative implementation view using XML and XQuery is provided as well.

4- It provides a flexible, yet systematic approach to the early requirements-based effort estimation, based on NFRs Ontology. It complementarily uses one standard functional size measurement model and a linear regression technique.

1.6 Outline of the Book

The rest of this book is organized as follows: Chapter 2 presents related work on existing approaches of treatments for NFRs in software engineering; Chapter 3 presents our research methodology. Chapter 4 presents the NFRs Ontology work. Chapter 5 proposes a traceability mechanism for change management of NFRs. Chapter 6 proposes a software effort estimation approach based on both FRs and NFRs. Chapter 7 concludes the book and discusses future research extensions.

Chapter II: Related Work on Early Treatment Methods of NFRs in Software Engineering

"Your true value depends entirely on what you are compared with."
Bob Wells (1966-)

2.1 Introduction

Most of the early work on NFRs focused on measuring how much a software system is in accordance with the set of NFRs that it should satisfy, using some form of quantitative analysis [Boe78], [FP97], [KKP90] and [Lyu96] offering predefined metrics to assess the degree to which a given software object meets a particular NFR. Those approaches that are concerned with measuring how much software complies with NFRs are called product-oriented approaches. On the contrary, process-oriented approaches focus on the software development process. It aims to help software engineers searching for alternatives to sufficiently meet NFRs while developing the software.

Our major contribution presented in this book (see Chapter 1, Section 1.5) explores the NFRs under the umbrella of the process-oriented approaches. Instead of evaluating the final software product, the emphasis here is on trying to rationalize the development process itself in terms of NFRs for the purpose of characterizing them, improving their traceability and predict their effort at an early stage of the development process.

In this chapter, we will introduce three categories of related work of interest to treat NFRs earlier during the development process; namely: (i) NFR Framework, (ii) incorporating NFRs into UML models and (iii) Aspect-Orientation. These three categories are presented in sections 2.2, 2.3 and 2.4 of this chapter. We also present in Section 2.5 a comprehensive critique to the three major approaches. We make the note that the scope of the related work included in this chapter is generic and it includes approaches to incorporate NFRs into the earlier models of the software development process. The related work focused on the topics of NFRs conceptualization, NFRs traceability and NFRs effort estimation is provided separately in chapters 4, 5 and 6, correspondingly.

2.2 NFR Framework

The NFR framework [CNYM00] is a process-oriented and goal-oriented approach that is aimed at making NFRs explicit and putting them in the forefront in the stakeholder's mind. It requires the following interleaved tasks, which are iterative:

Task 1. Acquiring knowledge about the system's domain, FRs and the particular kinds of NFRs for a particular system;

Task 2. Identifying NFRs as NFR softgoals and decomposing them into a finer level;

Task 3. Identifying the possible design alternatives for meeting NFRs in the target system as operationalizing softgoals;

Task 4. Dealing with ambiguities, tradeoffs, priorities and interdependencies among NFRs and operationalizations;

Task 5. Selecting operationalizations;

Task 6. Supporting decisions with a design rationale;

Task 7. Evaluating the impact of operationalization selection decisions on NFR satisfaction.

A cornerstone of this framework is the concept of the "softgoal", which is used to represent the NFR. A softgoal is a goal that has no-clear cut definition or criteria to determine whether or not it has been satisfied. In fact, the framework speaks of softgoals being "satisficed" rather than satisfied, to underscore their ad hoc nature, both with respect to their definition and to their satisfaction. The term "satisfice" was coined by Herbert Simon [Sim81]. Satisficing is a decision-making strategy that attempts to meet criteria for adequacy, rather than to identify an optimal solution.

The operation of the framework can be visualized in terms of the incremental and interactive construction, elaboration, analysis and revision of a softgoal interdependency graph (SIG). Figure 2-1 presents an example of a SIG with NFR softgoals representing requirements for performance and security of customer accounts in a credit card system. In the SIG, all softgoals are given *Type[Topic1, Topic2,...]* nomenclature. For the NFR softgoal, *Type* indicates the NFR concern and *Topic* indicates the NFR context.

NFRs softgoals are depicted by a cloud in the SIG. Architects further refine the NFRs into a suitable set of NFR softgoals. In doing so, they aim to find solutions in the target system that will satisfice the NFR softgoals. These solutions are called operationalizations, and are depicted by clouds with a thick border. High-level softgoals are refined into more specific subgoals or operationalizations. In each refinement, the offspring can contribute fully or partially, and positively or negatively, towards satisficing the parent. In Figure 2-1, both *space* and *response time* should be satisficed for the performance to be satisficed. The AND contribution is represented by a single arc, and the OR by double arcs.

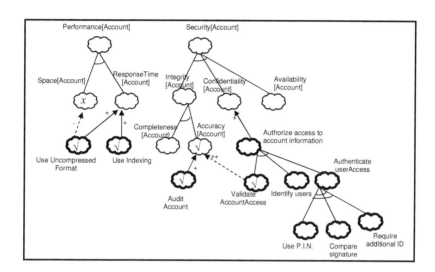

Figure 2-1: Softgoal Interdependency Graph for Performance and Security in a Credit Card System [CNYM00].

Other types of contributions are: MAKE (++), HELP (+), HURT (-) and BREAK (--). While making choices in pursuit of a particular softgoal, it is very likely that other softgoals may be affected in this decision-making process. This is shown with interdependencies among the softgoals (the dashed lines in the figure). For example, *UseUncompressedFormat* has a negative contribution with respect to *Space*.

During the evaluation step, which was labeled Task 7, the NFR framework applies propagation rules to determine to what extent the models satisfice the NFR softgoals. Some detailed propagation rules are given in [CNYM00]; however, the following simplified propagation rules (labeled R1 to R6) summarize Task 7.

R1. If most of the contributions received by a leaf NFR softgoal are positive (MAKE or HELP), then that leaf NFR softgoal is considered to be satisficed.

R2. If most of the contributions received by a leaf NFR softgoal are negative (BREAK or HURT), then that leaf NFR softgoal is considered to be denied or not satisficed.

R3. In the case of priority softgoals, or when there is a tie between positive and negative contributions, the system architect or the developer can make the design decision based on / or a variation of R1 and R2.

R4. In the case of the AND contribution, if all the child's softgoals are satisficed then the parent NFR softgoal is satisficed; otherwise, the parent's softgoal is denied.

R5. In the case of the OR contribution, if at least one child softgoal is satisficed, then the parent NFR softgoal is satisficed; otherwise, the parent softgoal is denied.

R6. In the case of a refinement (only one child), the parent is satisficed if the child is satisficed; and the parent is denied if the child is denied.

2.3 Incorporating NFRs with UML Models

In [MAB02], [PKL04], [AMBR02] and many others; early integration of NFRs is accomplished by extending UML models to integrate NFRs to the functional behavior.

Supakkul *et al.* propose a use case and goal-driven approach to integrate FRs and NFRs in [SC04]. They use the UML use case model to capture functionality of the system and they also use the NFR Framework [CNYM00] to represent NFRs. They propose to associate the NFRs with four use case model elements: *actor, use case, actor-use case association* and the *system boundary*. They name these associations "Actor Association Point", "Use Case Association Point", "Actor-Use Case Association (AU-A) Point", and "System Boundary Association Point" respectively. Having such an extension to the UML use case model, NFRs can be integrated at the requirements analysis level with FRs and can provide better understanding of the requirements model. Figure 2-2 shows the proposed NFR association points in the UML use case model. In Figure 2-2, cloud "A" represents the NFRs related to an *actor* of a use case model. These NFRs are related to *actor* by "Actor Association Point". For example, associating scalability NFR to Customer actor would indicate that the system must handle potentially large number of users accessing system functionality represented by use cases available to the actor. Cloud "B" represents the NFRs related to *use case* of use case model. These NFRs are related to *use case* by "Use Case Association Point". For example, associating fast response time NFR to Withdraw Fund use case of an Automated Teller Machine (ATM) system would indicate that the system must complete the functionality described by the Withdraw Fund use case within an acceptable duration. Cloud "C" represents the NFRs related to *actor-use case association* of the use case model. These NFRs are related to this association by "Actor-Use Case Association (AU-

A) Point". For example, associating security NFR to an AU-A between Customer and Withdraw Fund use case would indicate that withdraw fund must be secured, which also precisely implies that user interface to other AU-A not required to be secured. Finally, cloud "D" represents the NFRs related to *system boundary* of use case model. These NFRs are related to this boundary by "System Boundary Association Point". For example, associating portability NFR to the system boundary would intuitively specify that the NFR is global and that the system must be operational in multiple platforms, which globally affects every part of the system. These four NFRs association points are the authors' proposed extensions to the UML use case model.

Moreira et al. [MAB02] and [AMBR02] propose three main activities for integrating crosscutting quality attributes with FRs: identify, specify and integrate requirements, so that separation of concerns at the requirements level can be achieved. Firstly, identify all the requirements of a system and select from those the quality attributes relevant to the application domain and stakeholders. Secondly, specify FRs, using a use case based approach, and describe quality attributes using special templates including fields of: *description, focus, source, decomposition, priority, obligation,* and *influence*. Finally, those quality attributes are integrated with FRs using standard UML diagrammatic representations (e.g. use case diagram, interaction diagrams) extended with some special notations.

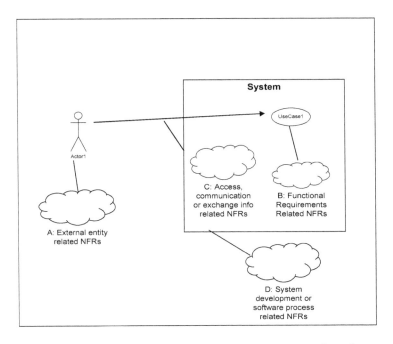

Figure 2-2: NFR Association Points in a Use-Case Diagram [SC04].

Cysneiros et al. [CLN01], [CL01] and [NLC00] propose a new strategy that brings NFRs to object-oriented modeling called OONFR (Object-Oriented Non Functional Requirement). They use the Language Extended Lexicon (LEL) driven approach to describe the application domain in LEL to provide context for both FRs and NFRs. This policy assures that a common and controlled vocabulary will be used in both functional and nonfunctional representations. Later the authors analyze those domains separately and build the functional view of the system using UML diagrams. Then they build the non-functional view of the system using NFR framework (see Section 2.2 of this chapter). They extend the NFR framework to adopt their notations. Finally, they integrate the NFRs with the functional representation of the system by proposing some extensions to UML models (use case diagram, class diagram, sequence diagram and communication diagram).

Dimitrov et al. [DSD02] analyze three UML-based approaches to performance modeling: 1) Directly representing performance aspects with UML and transferring effective model diagrams into corresponding performance models, 2) Expanding UML (use case diagram and state machine diagram) to deal with performance aspects and 3) Combining UML with formal description techniques such as Specification and Description Logic (SDL) and Message Sequence Charts (MSCs).

Berenbach et al. [BG06] from Siemens Corporation suggest from the experience with outsourcing and off shoring that use of graphical languages significantly reduces cultural and communication problems when teams (e.g. analysis and design) are at different locations. They propose an extension of UML use case model with new notations: i) as a starting point for an unified modeling approach, ii) to support the integration of hazard and requirement analysis and the binding of the resultant exposed requirements to their respective use cases, as well as iii) the binding of use cases to the high level features of a developed feature model.

In [ZG07], the authors propose a UML profile for modeling design decisions and an associated UML profile for modeling NFRs in a generic way. The two UML profiles consider design decisions and NFRs as first class elements. This relationship between design decisions and NFRs is modeled using specialized dependency notations in UML.

In [Jur02], the author proposes UMLsec which is an extension of UML notation. UMLsec allows expressing security relevant information within the diagrams in a system specification. UMLsec is defined in form of a UML profile using the standard UML extension mechanisms. In particular, the associated constraints give criteria to evaluate the security aspects of a system design, by referring to a formal semantics of asimplified fragment of UML.

In [LBD02], the authors present a modeling language, based on UML, called SecureUML. It shows how UML can be used to specify information related to access control in the overall design of an application and how this information can be used to automatically generate complete access control infrastructures. The work in [LBD02] adapts use cases to capture and analyze security requirements. This adaptation is called an Abuse Case Model. An abuse case is defined as a specification of a type of complete interaction between a system and one or more actors, where the results of the interaction are harmful to the system, one of the actors, or one of the stakeholders of the system.

Figure 2-3 summarizes the related work presented in this section to incorporate NFRs against all types of UML 2.0 diagrams.

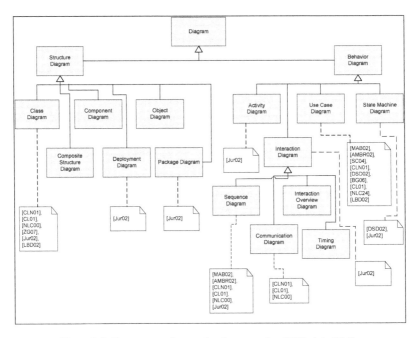

Figure 2-3: Summary to Approaches Incorporating NFRs into UML.

2.4 Treating NFRs with Aspect Orientation

A software system is the realization of a set of concerns which are the primary motivation for organizing and decomposing software into manageable and comprehensible parts. Concerns come from a variety of sources, for example clients, developers, managers, administrators, firmware or hardware portions of a system and business context. Different viewpoints can have the same concerns, but the associated requirements may differ. For example, in a banking application, the teller and loan officer may be concerned about access control. For a teller, the requirement maybe "teller should not access loan information". For loan officer the requirement maybe "loan officer should not manipulate loan amount". Even though both view points have access control concern, the requirements are different.

When Object-Oriented Programming (OOP) entered the mainstream of software development, it had a great impact on how software was developed as developers tackle larger systems with less time by modeling their concerns as groups of interacting objects and classes, which are generally derived from the entities in the requirements specification and use-cases. However, OOP is essentially static as a change in requirements can have an implication on development timelines. As discussed in the previous chapter, some requirements like NFRs need to be addressed in multiple modules of the system or they may need to be addressed in the system as a whole. Consequently, the code to handle these requirements may be mixed in with the core logic of a huge number of modules, resulting in bad implications on the software quality.

Despite the success of object-orientation in the effort to achieve separation of concerns, current OOP techniques support one dimensional decomposition of the problem focusing on the notion of a class. Such decomposition is not a good candidate to handle complex interaction of components as it leaves certain properties without being localized in single modular units and as a result their implementation cuts across the decomposition of the system. This is the phenomenon of crosscutting.

Aspect-Oriented Programming (AOP) is a new programming paradigm that allows programmers to separate concerns and thus allows them to dynamically modify the static behavior of the object-oriented model. Just as objects in the real world can change their states during their lifecycles, an application can adopt new characteristics as it develops. AOP provides a solution for abstracting crosscutting code that spans object hierarchies without functional relevance to the code it spans. Instead of embedding crosscutting code in classes, AOP allows to abstract the crosscutting code into a separate module (known as an aspect). Then, AOP provides special rules of composition between components and aspects. For the necessary background on AOP, we advise the reader to visit the background chapter (Chapter 2) in our earlier work [Kaso6].

While AOP supports separation of concerns at the code level, Aspect-Oriented Software Development (AOSD) has extended AOP to provide a systematic support for the identification, separation, representation (through proper modeling and documentation), and composition of crosscutting concerns as well as mechanism that make them traceable throughout software development.

Although, initially the focus was merely on aspects at the programming level, recently a considerable amount of research has been focusing to identify and model aspects in the early phases of software development. Because of the crosscutting nature of NFRs, these requirements are good candidates to be treated with aspect-orientation.

However, current aspect-oriented approaches either concentrate on serving as a general purpose architecture modeling language within a particular domain, or support the analysis of one specific NFR of a system (e.g., performance or security) in a way that is not necessarily applicable to other NFRs and with ignorance to possible existence of crosscutting FRs. In addition, these approaches do not fully support a smooth transition among the requirements, analysis and the design phases.

In [RMA03] and [RSMA02] the authors propose an approach for modularizing and composing crosscutting concerns. The approach involves identifying requirements using stakeholder' viewpoints, use-cases/scenarios, goals or problem frames. The approach basically uses a set of matrices consisting of viewpoints and concerns represented in XML. Even though the authors show that some NFRs can crosscut viewpoint specifications, it is not clear how NFRs arise. The identification of the dimension of a candidate aspect (its influence on certain aspects of the system) is not performed in a systematic way in this work. Scenarios tend to be treated as single modules (or black boxes) that have to be composed with crosscutting concerns. However, simple composition rules between scenarios and crosscutting requirements cannot be always applicable as relationships between them are normally not clean-cut, this approach does not show the propagation of a scenario into a potentially large set of components inside analysis and design and the (normally complex) rules of composition between individual components and aspects. In fact, the influence of a single aspect policy on different sets of components that collectively implement the same scenario may be different. Similarly, the same aspect may influence the same set of components in a number of different ways. In addition, in this approach, resolving conflicts among concerns is recommended through negotiation with stakeholders, which may not always be applicable as; with the exception of developers, stakeholders are not interested in system concerns and they may not have the necessary expertise to be involved in these matters. They would merely want their requirements implemented.

In [BM04], the authors propose an approach to identify and compose crosscutting concerns. The approach consists of four defined steps: identify concerns, specify concerns, identify crosscutting concerns and compose concerns. The composition of concerns is defined using the formal method LOTOS. The approach focuses on the requirements analysis phase, and contains no traceability support to other phases of the software development life cycle. It is not clear how we can map the LOTOS specification to the design and the implementation components. Resolving conflicts among concerns is recommended through negotiation with stakeholders, which may not always be applicable as we discussed earlier. The approach recommends defining a dominant concern among the crosscutting concerns at certain joinpoint. The notion of a dominant concern cannot always be applicable. In complex systems (such as concurrent systems) two or more aspects may affect the same joinpoints with changing priorities to the execution of the behavior of some component (e.g. method body), so assigning a hard-coded prioritization will not follow the correct semantics.

In [CDDD03], the authors provide an approach to support one NFR, namely performance, under the umbrella of AOSD using the UML and the formal architectural description language Rapide. Although the authors describe how they plan to extend their approach to support two or more NFRs, it is an open issue how to consider crosscutting FRs within their solution.

In [TBB04], the authors adopt model analysis to detect semantic conflicts between aspects. The authors introduce two levels of conflicts among aspects:

1. Direct conflict: two or more aspects sharing the same joinpoint or an aspect is having a joinpoint in another aspect.

2. Indirect conflict: the aspects don not share a common joinpoint but one aspect can have an impact on the behavior of the second. This approach is dedicated to serve the detection of direct conflicts only. Resolving conflicts is recommended through a process of correction and refinement of the model, which is not clearly investigated.

In [BB99] and [MRG+04] the obliviousness property was adopted to model orthogonal aspects independently from each other and from the FRs. The deployment of formal methods in these approaches (e.g. GAMMA, LOTOS, Time Temporal Logic) to specify the functional behavior and the associated aspects helps to enable formal validation and facilitates a specification-driven design. On the other hand, the weaving process is not presented in a precise systematic way and it is limited to a specific type of requirements that could not necessary be applicable for others. In addition, it is not clear where and how the formalism is to be placed within the AOSD framework or how to integrate it with the traditional iterative development process.

In [NAB04], the authors reason about the semantics of the composition mechanisms of the programming language through an approach that is based on a single meta-model: Composition Graphs meta-model. While these graphs may provide a sufficient homogeneous comprehension for the semantics among different programming languages that make them easier to compare and to be transformed, the process to construct such graphs without existing tools can be tedious. In addition, the graphs are generated from an existing implementation that we don not usually have when we initially develop the application.

Park et al. [PKL04] propose a simulation based design phase analysis method based on aspect oriented programming. In his method, quality aspects remain separate from functionality aspect in the design model. The functionality concern and the performance concern are weaved by the AspectJ compiler. For the purpose of presenting the method, the authors show a sequence diagram overlaid with AspectJ elements. Lines of Code for performance analysis are inserted before or after appropriate pointcuts in the diagram.

Xu et al. [XZRL05] propose a conceptual architectural design model, where traditional architecture model of a software program represents one layer and the NFRs are presented as aspectual components in another layer. Figure 2-4 shows their conceptual design model to add NFRs. They propose to use the aspectual components to represent the semantics of the operationalized NFRs. These components correspond to advice tasks in the aspect-oriented world. The connectors between the software architecture layer and the NFR layer describe binding rules, thus corresponding to the pointcut from the aspectual component to the normal components. They also define a connector, namely XML Binder, to bind the NFRs to the target model. They propose to use the same XML Binders in the Aspect Markup Language (AML). Their XML Binders are therefore XML-based binding specifications that provide weaving instructions to determine how aspectual components and the traditional software architecture are to be composed together.

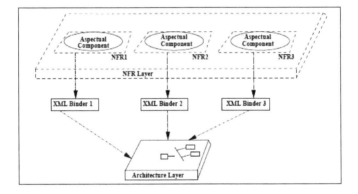

Figure 2-4: Conceptual Design Model with One Architecture.

In order to fill the missing gaps in the above discussed AOSD approaches, we presented in [KCO05], [KO06] and [Kaso6] a systematic and precisely defined aspect-oriented model towards an early consideration of specifying and separating crosscutting FRs and NFRs. Our proposed model is depicted in Figure 2-5. The model is composed of five phases: Requirements Elicitation, Analysis and Crosscutting Realization, Composing Requirements, Design and Implementation. We use the term phase to describe a group of one or more activities within the model. The phase is a mean to categorize activates based on the general target they tend to achieve. These phases contribute towards the target solution to establish a mechanism for integrating NFRs during requirements engineering and architectural design. Requirements traceability is provided throughout the model to influence the consistency and change management of the requirements of a system. This is achieved in our model by using two hierarchy graphs to keep track of the required behavior of the system using static and dynamic views of objects starting from requirements elicitation till the implementation. We referred to the graphs by the static and the dynamic hierarchies. The hierarchies are introduced and updated at certain breakpoints within the development process as follows:

1. End of Requirements Elicitation phase: The dynamic hierarchy is introduced. At this phase, we are supposed to have successfully specified the use-cases through scenarios that constitute as the origin for the dynamic behavior of the system.

2. End of Analysis and Crosscutting Realization phase: The static hierarchy is introduced. At this phase, we are supposed to have defined the conceptual classes (through the domain model) that constitute the origin of the static behavior of the system. The dynamic hierarchy is updated to show the effect of crosscutting realization among use-cases.

3. End of Composing Requirements phase: The static hierarchy is updated to show the effect of integrating NFRs with the conceptual classes.

4. End of Design Phase: Both hierarchies are updated to show the extension to the design level through the static artifacts (e.g. class diagram) and dynamic artifacts (e.g. communication diagram).

In [OKCo5] and [KOCo5], we proposed sets of quality measurements to be associated with activities of the AOSD model. The intended goal of the measurements is to assist stakeholders with quantitative evidences to better map or iterate system modules at different activities in the development process and to better set the design decisions for the analyzed requirements.

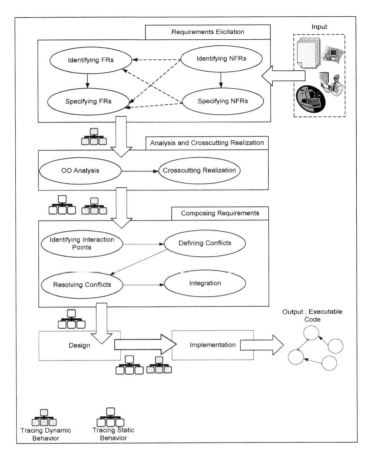

Figure 2-5: Proposed Model to integrate NFRs early in the software development process [Kas06] and [KO06].

2.5 Discussion

The tendency to treat NFRs as softgoals in the NFR framework can often add ambiguity to the requirements specifications. For example, the response time in a user interface is typically soft, whereas response time requirements in real-time systems can be hard. This situation calls for extending the taxonomy of the NFR framework so that it can identify those NFRs that need to be stated in terms of crisp indicators and their acceptable values.

Another major drawback in the NFR framework is the lack of a formal definition towards how NFRs are associated with other entities of the system throughout the development process. This drawback makes the NFRs framework not a reasonable vehicle towards discussing NFRs traceability and effort estimation. In addition, NFRs framework offers only a qualitative not quantitative treatment of NFRs.

In addition, there is no numerical evaluation on the usage of the NFRs framework. The authors demonstrate the applicability of the proposed tasks through a case study. Our critique discussion on the limitation of the NFR framework was published in [KDO07a].

While the AOSD approaches (including our previous work [KCO05], [KO06], [Kas06]) aim at addressing the crosscutting nature of NFRs, current AOSD approaches come short when addressing the other elements that characterize the nature of NFRs (e.g. subjectivity and interactivity). In addition, AOSD approaches map the crosscutting concern towards the aspect element in the implemented code space. This is in fact not a sufficient solution for every type of NFR as some of these requirements may be mapped to an architectural decision and not to an implemented code. Most AOSD approaches rely on case studies to demonstrate the applicability of their work.

In [MAB02], [PKL04], [AMBR02] and many others; early integration of NFRs is accomplished by extending UML models to integrate NFRs to the functional behavior. Although the composition process must be considered at the meta-level, these approaches only model certain NFRs (e.g. response time, security) in a way that is not necessarily applicable for other requirements. There is no single existing formal method available that is well suited for defining and analyzing numerous NFRs for a system. Evaluation of approaches under this category is either missing or relying on a case study to demonstrate the applicability.

Based on the pervious review, we are motivated to fill the gap raised from the previously open problems. In order to be able to represent and reason about NFRs, we need to access a formal representation that is capable to accommodate the wide range of these requirements. In the next chapter, we will describe our research methodology and its demonstrated applicability.

Chapter III: Research Methodology

"If the only tool you have is a hammer, you tend to see every problem as a nail."
Abraham Maslow (1908 – 1970).

3.1 Introduction

The research approach used in this book includes three major phases. These are described in Section 3.2 of this chapter. We refer to phase as a group of one or more activities. The phase is a mean to categorize research activities based on the general target they tend to achieve. The practical applicability of the approach has been investigated and demonstrated in this book by using three case studies and one controlled experiment. The case studies are described in Section 3.3. Section 3.4 refers the reader to the applicability of the outcomes of this work.

3.2 Methodology

Figure 3-1 summarizes the complete research methodology, which consists of three major phases:

1. Building a formal model for NFRs and their relations (Chapter 4).
2. Implementing changes management mechanism for tracing impact of NFRs on other constructs in the ontology and vice versa (Chapter 5).
3. Proposing a novel approach to the early requirements-based effort estimation, based on NFRs Ontology (Chapter 6).

Three evaluation phases are included in our methodology to demonstrate the validity and applicability of each of the above major phases. In each of the evaluation phases, the common research question that is addressed is: *"How does our proposed method improve existing practice? What are the implications of our method for practitioners in requirements engineering?"*

The outcome of each evaluation phase serves as input towards improvement of the outcome of the precedent phase. The three major phases are described next.

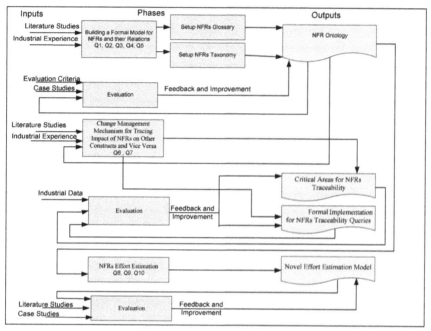

Figure 3-1: Research Methodology

3.2.1 Phase 1: Building a Formal Model for NFRs and their Relations

This phase started with the exploratory activities of the project to investigate the nature of the NFRs and previous research on the areas defined in the problem statement section (Chapter 1, Section 1.2). During this phase we also collected evidence about practices in industry which refers to the integration of NFRs into the software engineering process and practices that architects use in transforming NFRs into architecture. The research activities in this phase formed three steps: the first step was to shape the problem domain by understanding the context around it. The second step was to collect knowledge on what practical solutions architects currently are using to confront the issues in the problem domain. The third step was to assess in which respects the current solutions come short and how big existing requirements engineering and architectural design gap is in respect to NFRs. Throughout this process, we built experiences in how to improve the current practices of transformation from requirements to architecture with respect to NFRs.

In this phase, we used literature studies, surveys, and experiences gained at industrial sites, to answer five exploratory and correlational [ESSD07] research questions:

Q1- What is a NFR?

Q2-What are the types of NFRs? How can they be categorized?

Q3- How does NFR interact with FRs and their refinements during the software development process?

Q4- How does one NFR interact with other NFRs?

Q5- What are the concepts and relationships which characterize the interactions referred to in Q3 and Q4?

The process of finding the answers to these questions represents an observational and descriptive study for the nature of NFRs. The unit of analysis at this research phase is, therefore, the NFR from the perspective of process-oriented approaches. The answers to these questions resulted in a clearer understanding of the nature of NFRs, including more precise definitions of the related theoretical terms. In this book, we turned the findings from answering the above questions into a formal model for NFRs and their relations. The model was captured though a Common Foundation for NFRs which is realized by developing the NFRs Ontology. The ontology represents the outcome of this phase. The applicability of the proposed ontology was evaluated through the three case studies presented in Section 3.3 of this chapter and which were performed with both students and professionals (experts) in the domain of our study.

Our work in this phase has been published in [KDO07a], [KOD07b], [DKPWO07], [KOD09b], [SOKH09] and [KOD10].

3.2.2 Phase 2: Changes Management Mechanism for Tracing Impact of NFRs on Other Constructs in the Ontology and vice versa

This phase represents our first usage of the NFRs Ontology as a vehicle towards supporting those requirements engineering activities that pertain to NFRs. The "Descriptive Process" [ESSD07] research questions we address here are:

Q6: What traceability mechanisms are used in theory and practice to support requirements engineering and architectural design decisions for NFRs? What complexity aspects of NFRs are accounted for in current requirements engineering and architectural design decision-making processes?

Q7: What are the critical areas requiring traceability attention when dealing with change management of NFRs? How are these areas mapped to the concepts and relationships defined in the NFRs Ontology?

The research in this phase represents an observational and correlational study. The outcome of this phase is a formal implementation of the answers derived from Q7. The applicability of the implementation was evaluated by a multi-project variation experiment [BSH86] and [Bas96] that was conducted with experts from NOKIA – Montreal under normal work conditions (vivo). Our work in this phase has been published in [KO06], [KOD08a], [KOD09a] and [KOD10].

3.2.3 Phase 3: NFRs Effort Estimation

This phase uses a view of the NFRs Ontology and deploys it for the aim of establishing an approach towards an early effort estimation of development of the software project taking into account both FRs and NFRs. The research questions we address in this phase are:

Q8: What is the impact of NFRs on the total effort for building and maintaining the software project?

Q9: In which ways are NFRs treated in current theoretical and practical effort estimation models?

Q10: How to improve the existing practice of early estimation for the effort taking into account the impact of NFRs?

The outcome of this phase is a novel effort estimation model that aims at better prediction of the effort for building the project from the given set of FRs and NFRs.

We followed the case study approach as an investigation technique to evaluate the work of this phase (see Section 3.3.2 of this chapter). We make the note that for the purpose of evaluation, we considered the option of carrying out a formal experiment, however this choice (as an alternative to the case study approach) was eliminated because there is not much theory in the field, and what theory there is, is mostly qualitative; and also because there are so many state variables that influence the evaluation results and that it can not be replicated easily.

Our work in this phase has been published in [KDO07], [KODo7a], [KODo8b], [KODo8c], [KDO09] and [KOD10].

3.3 Case Studies

The selection of cases is a crucial step in case study research. The aim is to select cases that are most relevant to the study proposition. Multiple case studies design usually offer greater validity [ESSD07]. We have selected three case studies that will help to (i) illustrate the discussion and (ii) provide the necessary evaluation.

3.3.1 NOKIA Mobile Email Application System

The Mobile Email application, which provides the context for our discussion, consists of the NOKIA Mobile Email Gateway and the NOKIA Mobile Email Client. The high-level context diagram of the application is presented in Figure 3-2. The NOKIA Mobile Email Client provides the user interface. Using recognizable and branded email portals (e.g. Yahoo, MSN, etc.), the mobile email experience mirrors the familiar 'look and feel' of the PC, generating instant consumer adoption and virtually eliminating the learning curve.

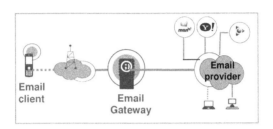

Figure 3-2: Mobile Email Solution

The Mobile Email Gateway provides mobile operators with the necessary protocol adaptations, billing, reporting, and customer care interfaces they require to effectively deliver branded portal email services to their subscribers. As a result, mobile operators can increase their average revenue per user and directly impact their bottom line with a variety of flexible billing options. Communication between the client and the gateway is established through a SYNCML protocol, which is an XML-based standard for data synchronization.

The settings from this case study were used to provide the illustration for the three major phases of this research. In addition, these settings have been used for the evaluation purposes of phases 1 and 2.

3.3.2 IEEE Montreal Website

The second case study has been conducted with the teams of the undergraduate students in their third year of studies enrolled in the 2009 "Software Measurement" and "Software Project" undergraduate SOEN courses at Concordia University, Montreal, Canada. The project required all groups of students to develop a new website for the IEEE-Montreal chapter. The IEEE System software is custom designed and built to meet the needs of one specific customer – the Montreal section of the IEEE. All significant aspects of the system that users may access or manipulate have been specified by the customer, as well as some aspects of the system's architecture, performance and security. The system has a client-server design. Users access the system from a remote terminal that is connected to the main computer via an internet link. The system can function as an independent unit but has the option of connecting to other systems and services provided by the IEEE.

The IEEE System software is both an administrative support system and an information system. It is accessed through a simple GUI hosted in a web browser. Any internet-enabled computer with a web browser can access the system and multiple concurrent users are supported.

A primary goal of the system is to provide an easy to navigate interface for both casual and administrative users. The UI is available in both English and French. News and information about IEEE events are prominently displayed. The administrative parts of the site are protected against un-authorized access.

The settings from this study were used to provide an additional evaluation for phase 1 and the core evaluation for phase 3.

3.3.3 SAP Project

The third case study has been conducted with an expert in a leading Enterprise Resource Planning (ERP) software producer, SAP. Currently, the need for the SAP project management is still requesting more efficient methodologies and techniques to assist the project manager during the project estimation. SAP implementation is one of the large markets that still have challenge to have a close quantification of different project parameters regarding the real need of implementation projects. In this case study, the SAP expert instantiated the NFRs Ontology using a set of requirements from one of their major SAP projects. The purpose of the project is to replace the old version of SAP and other legacy systems in order to integrate all the business processes within the same ERP.

The settings of this case study were used to provide an additional evaluation for phase 1 of this research.

3.4 Applicability

The applicability of the approaches resulting from this research has been demonstrated by (i) improving the NFRs specification (see Chapter 4, Section 4.7), (ii) improving the testing practices for NFR on deployed software using the proposed traceability mechanism (see Chapter 5, Section 5.6) and (iii) better predicting the effort for building the software project taking the impact of NFRs into consideration (see Chapter 6, Section 6.6).

Chapter IV: An Ontology Based approach to Non-Functional Requirements Conceptualization

"The first step towards wisdom is calling things by their right names."
Chinese Proverb

4.1 Introduction

The growing interest in ontology-based applications as opposed to systems based on information models have resulted in an increasing interest in the definition of conceptual models for any kind of domain. Software engineering is one of those domains that have received high attention in that respect [MA04], [SC05] and [WADD03]. Current research studies by Knowledge Engineering scholars on requirement acquisition, for example, use domain ontology to support software requirements description [HM06], [Jin00] and [KS05]. These studies leverage the existing knowledge of the relationship between the software requirements and the information in the related domain. According to this relationship, the domain knowledge influences the result of requirements acquisition [JKCW08]. International Software Engineering standards such as IEEE [IEEE6101290] provide a foundation for the development of ontology for software engineering in terms of common vocabulary and concepts. Nonetheless, the process of analysis of the standards to come up with a logical coherent ontology is by no means a simple process [SC05]. Moreover, the NFRs have received little or no attention from the ontology research groups due to inherent challenges imposed by the semantic imprecision of NFRs conceptual schemas [SC05].

Existing NFRs elicitation methods adopt memo of interview transcripts to collect initial NFRs and then construct systems with the NFRs integrated according to the experience and intuition of the designers [JKCW08]. However, empirical reports [BLF99], [FD96] and [LT93] indicated a number of drawbacks when not dealing with NFRs using systematic and well-defined methods. For example, a significant portion of NFRs may be neglected as it is difficult to ask users to provide their NFRs explicitly because they are always related to other concepts in the domain and affected by context. Furthermore, NFRs can often interact, in the sense that attempts to achieve one NFR can help or hinder the achievement of other NFRs at certain functionality. Such an interaction creates an extensive network of interdependencies and trade-offs between NFRs which is not easy to describe [CNYM00].

The growing awareness of these issues among the requirements engineering community in the last few years led to a heightened interest in NFRs description and modeling and, in turn, to the emergence of several models intended to capture and structure the more relevant concepts defining the NFRs and their relations. Such models are generic ones and must be instantiated to be usable for specific domains or applications. Yet, the instantiation process is not easy to perform since the generic models usually do not contain sufficient information about NFRs interdependencies [SBMB06]. Some standards have been proposed in order to unify the definition of subsets of NFRs; e.g., software quality concepts [ISO912601]. However, till now there is no clear and coherent generic representation of the NFRs concepts.

Building on the above discussion, a knowledge-based representation is necessary to support the description of NFRs within a system and to provide practitioners and researchers with a valuable alternative to current requirements engineering techniques. The aim of our research reported in this chapter is to systematically develop an ontology which provides the definition of the general concepts relevant to NFRs without reference to any particular application domain. The general concepts can then act as a common foundation for describing particular non-functional attributes as well as providing a conceptual model for NFRs (including e.g. entity definitions, relations, etc.). The ontology also contains rules which define the semantics of the defined concepts.

The rest of this chapter is organized as follows: Section 4.2 provides the necessary background on ontologies in software engineering and the Web Ontology Language (OWL). Section 4.3 describes the common foundation development process. Section 4.4 discusses the development of the terminological level of the NFRs Ontology, while Section 4.5 discusses the conceptual level. Section 4.6 discusses the evaluation phase of the NFRs Ontology. Section 4.7 presents related work. Section 4.8 concludes the chapter.

4.2 Background

4.2.1 Ontologies in Software Engineering

Ontology can be defined as "*a specification of a* conceptualization" [Gru93]. More precisely, ontology is an explicit formal specification of how to represent the objects, concepts, and other entities that exist in some area of interest and the relationships that hold among them. In general, for ontology to be useful, it must represent a shared, agreed upon conceptualization.

The use of ontologies in computing has gained popularity in recent years for two main reasons: i) they facilitate interoperability and ii) they facilitate machine reasoning.

In its simplest form, ontology is taxonomy of domain terms. However, taxonomies by themselves are of little use in machine reasoning. The term ontology also implies the modeling of domain rules. It is these rules, which provide an extra level of machine "understanding".

Ontologies are already used to aid research in a number of fields [SOKH09] and [GKM08]. They are often used in the development of thesauri which need to model the relationships between nodes. One example is the National Cancer Institute Thesaurus [NCI03], which contains over 500,000 nodes covering information ranging from disease diagnosis to the drugs, techniques and treatments used in cancer research.

Recently, the software engineering community has recognized ontologies as a promising way to address current software engineering problems [CFM06] and [HS06]. Researchers have so far proposed many different synergies between software engineering and Ontologies. For example, ontologies are proposed to be used in requirements engineering [LG05], software modeling [Knu04], model transformations [KKK+06], software maintenance [KBT07], software comprehension [WZR07], software methodologies [CH06], and software community of practice [ASHKW06].

The constructs used to create ontologies vary between ontology languages. One class of ontology languages is those which are based upon description logics [BHS03]. OWL is one such language. OWL is discussed in the following section as an illustration of how ontology may be created.

4.2.2 OWL

OWL [OWL] is the Web Ontology Language, an XML-based language for publishing and sharing ontologies via the web. OWL originated from DAML+OIL both of which are based on RDF (Resource Description Framework) triples. There are three 'species' of OWL – but the most useful for reasoning - OWL-DL - corresponds to a description logic.

OWL ontology consists of Classes; also referred to as concepts, and their Properties; also referred to by relations. The Class definition specifies the conditions for individuals to be members of a Class. A Class can therefore be viewed as a set. The set membership conditions are usually expressed as restrictions on the Properties of a Class. For instance the *allValuesFrom* and *someValuesFrom* property restrictions commonly occur in Class definitions. These correspond to the universal quantifier ($\forall$) and existential quantifier ($\exists$) of predicate logic. More precisely, in OWL such restrictions form anonymous Classes of all individuals matching the corresponding predicate.

Classes may be constructed from other Classes using the *intersectionOf*, *unionOf* and *complementOf* constructs which correspond to their namesakes from set theory. Another way to define a Class is to specify all individuals of which it consists explicitly using the one of construct. A key feature of OWL and other description logics is that classification (and subsumption relationships) can be automatically computed by a reasoner which is a piece of software able to infer logical consequences from a set of asserted facts or axioms. For the purpose of the NFRs Ontology, we will use a semantic web reasoning system and information repository: Renamed Abox and Concept Expression Reasoner (RACER) [RACER]. An 'open world' assumption is made. This means that no assumptions are made about anything which is not asserted explicitly. One outcome of this is that a Class definition does not act as a template for individuals as it might in a closed world. For instance, an individual may have extra Properties about which nothing is asserted in its Class definition. An individual may also be a member of many Classes. Because classifications can be inferred, the creator of an individual does not need to be aware of all possible Classes into which the individual may fall at the time of creation. Instead, all Classes of which it is a member can be inferred by a reasoner. This is of a particular help for hierarchies of quality requirements which have been identified in the literature with more than one parent quality requirement (see Section 4.5.2.1.1).

The following snippet from our ontology gives a flavor of OWL. It defines a Class *MeasurableNonFunctionalRequirement*, stating that it is exactly equivalent to the *NonFunctionalRequirement* Class intersected with the set of all individuals which have a Property "hasIndicator", with at least one value which is an "Indicator"; Finally it states that the class *MeasurableNonFunctionalRequirement* and *NonMeasurableNonFunctionalRequirement* are disjoint.

```xml
<?xml version="1.0" encoding="UTF-8"?>
<owl:Class rdf:about="#MeasurableNonFunctionalRequirement">
   <owl:equivalentClass>
     <owl:Class>
        <owl:intersectionOf rdf:parseType="Collection">
           <owl:Restriction>
             <owl:someValuesFrom rdf:resource="#Indicator"/>
             <owl:onProperty>
                <owl:InverseFunctionalProperty rdf:about="#hasIndicator"/>
             </owl:onProperty>
           </owl:Restriction>
           <owl:Class rdf:about="#NonFunctionalRequirement"/>
        </owl:intersectionOf>
     </owl:Class>
```

```
    </owl:equivalentClass>
    <owl:disjointWith>
        <owl:Class rdf:ID="NonMeasurableNonFunctionalRequirement"/>
    </owl:disjointWith>
</owl:Class>
```

Clearly, this is not particularly human-readable, especially because the Classes and Properties referenced (*Indicator, hasIndicator, NonMeasurableNonFunctionalRequirement*) could be defined anywhere in the file. Editing OWL manually can be equally difficult for the very same reason. We used Protégé 3.3 [PROTÉGÉ] and its OWL plug-in for NFRs Ontology development. Figure 4-1 shows a snapshot from the NFRs Ontology built using the Protégé tool. Protégé is a free, open-source platform that provides a growing user community with a suite of tools to construct domain models and knowledge-based applications with ontologies. At its core, Protégé implements a rich set of knowledge-modeling structures and actions that support the creation, visualization, and manipulation of ontologies in various representation formats. Protégé can be customized to provide domain-friendly support for creating knowledge models and entering data.

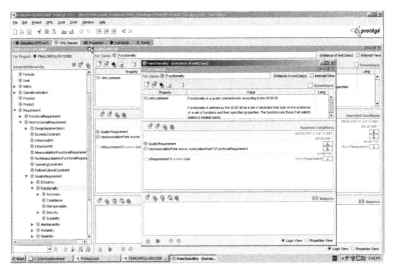

Figure 4-1: A Snapshot of the NFRs Ontology in Protégé.

4.3 Development Process of a Common Foundation

We need a disciplined process for the development of the NFRs common foundation; which will be realized by the NFRs Ontology. In the development of the Common Foundation we distinguish the following phases in the ontology development process: requirements for the ontology, design of the ontology, implementation of the ontology and evaluation of the ontology. There are supposed to be several iterations over these phases. In this section, we summarize the approach for the development of the NFRs Common Foundation. We describe the distinction between glossary and taxonomy. Furthermore, we introduce the deductive approach used in this process.

4.3.1 NFRs Ontology Requirements

In this section we list a number of requirements for the NFRs Common Foundation. The most important requirements are:

Req 1. The Common Foundation shall comprehensively represent common terminology and concepts used in NFRs (descriptive standard). This requirement states the main characteristic of the Common Foundation as a descriptive standard. The Common Foundation is not meant to be a prescriptive and normative standard.

These three types of standards can be described as follows [Sku02]:

- *Descriptive*: give definitions of facts.

- *Normative*: provide guidelines to be used as a basis for measurement, comparison or decision.

- *Prescriptive*: define a particular way of doing something.

Req 2. The Common Foundation shall be generally acceptable in order to facilitate communication between the partners and (re)use of terminology.

- *Generally accepted* means that the knowledge and practices described are applicable to most projects most of the time, and that there is widespread consensus about their value and usefulness. Generally accepted does not mean that the knowledge and practices described are or should be applied uniformly on all projects (adapted from Project Management Body of Knowledge [PMBOK00]).

Other captured requirements are:

Req 3. The Common Foundation shall be accurate, complete, conflict-free, and non-redundant. The characteristics of Req 3 are described by Shanks et al. [STW03] for validating conceptual models.

- *Accuracy.* The model should accurately represent the semantics of the domain as perceived by the focal stakeholder(s);

- *Completeness.* The model should completely represent the semantics of the domain as perceived by the focal stakeholder(s);

- *Conflict-free.* The semantics represented in different parts of the model should not contradict one another (also called consistency).

- *No redundancy.* To reduce the likelihood of conflicts arising if and when the model is subsequently updated the model should not contain redundant semantics (related to conciseness).

Req 4. The Common Foundation shall be unambiguous, verifiable, and traceable. The characteristics of Req 4 are also used for software requirements specifications [IEEE83098]:

- *Unambiguous.* The definition should only allow a single interpretation.

- *Verifiable.* The information can be checked for correctness.

- *Traceable.* The origin of the definition can be determined.

Req 5. The Common Foundation shall be usable: understandable, learnable, concise, and accessible.

Req 6. The Common Foundation shall be maintainable: analyzable, changeable (versions), testable and stable.

The characteristics of Req 5 and Req 6 are described in ISO/IEC 9126 [ISO912601], as software product quality (sub)characteristics. Usability and maintainability should be checked in the validation and deployment phases.

- *Maintainability.* The capability of the product to be modified.

- *Usability.* The capability of the product to be understood, learned, used and liked by the user, when used under specified conditions.

4.3.2 NFRs Ontology Design

In Noy et al. [NM00], several guidelines are given for ontology development. We will apply ontology engineering as used in the development of the Common Warehouse Metamodel (CWM) [CWM02]. The metamodel is described in the Unified Modeling Language (UML). In the CWM Business Nomenclature (see UML Class Diagram in Figure 4-2) two levels are distinguished:

- A *taxonomy* with *concepts* at semantic level (conceptual model or domain model),

- A *glossary* with *terms* at representation level (terminology).

A concept can be related to other concepts. The relation between concepts in a taxonomy can be generalization/specialization, aggregation and composition, association and dependency, where needed enriched with navigation direction, labels and multiplicities.

A concept is identified by a number of terms. A term can be related to other terms and can be used in the description of concepts. A term is described in its definition. There are many types of definitions such as denotative definitions, connotative definitions and operational definitions. In the NFRs Ontology, we will use denotative definitions. Those definitions rely on techniques that identify extension(s) of the general term being defined with the structure:

<Concept> is <more general concept> with <specific conditions>

Copi and Cohen [CC98] provide some *guidelines* for this type of definitions:

- Focus on essential properties.

- Avoid circularity.

- Capture correct properties (not too broad, not too narrow).

- Avoid ambiguous and figurative language; be factual, not persuasive.

- Be affirmative rather than negative.

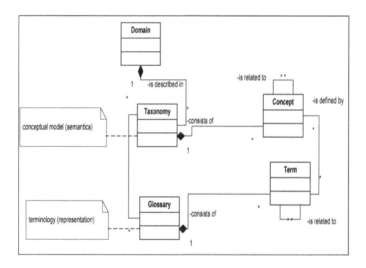

Figure 4-2: Relation Between Taxonomy and Glossary.

4.3.3 Deductive Approach

Holsapple [HJ02] describes a number of approaches to ontology design: inspiration, induction, deduction, synthesis and collaboration (See Table 4-1). We chose to follow the deductive approach.

Table 4-1: Approaches to Ontology Design.

Approach	Basis for Design
Inspiration	Individual viewpoint about the domain.
Induction	Specific case within the domain.
Deduction	General principles about the domain.
Synthesis	Set of existing models, each of which provides a partial characterization of the domain.
Collaboration	Multiple individuals' viewpoints about the domain, possibly coupled with an initial ontology as an anchor.

The deductive approach to ontology design is concerned with adopting some general principles and adaptively applying them to construct an ontology geared toward a specific case. This involves filtering and distilling the general notions so they are customized to a particular domain subset. It can also involve filling in details, effectively yielding an ontology that is an instantiation of the general notions.

For the purpose of developing the NFRs Ontology, we considered reusing existing ontologies; however, we could not find a relevant ontologies already existing so we started developing our ontology from scratch.

Most of the terms and concepts in use for describing NFRs have been loosely defined, and often there is no commonly accepted term for a general concept [Glio7]. As indicated in the Introduction (Section 4.1), Common Foundation is required to enable effective communication and to enable integration of activities within the RE community. This Common Foundation is realized by developing an ontology, i.e. the shared meaning of terms and concepts in the domain of NFRs. In Section 4.4, we discuss the terminological level of the NFRs Ontology, while in Section 4.5, we discuss the conceptual aspect of the NFRs Ontology.

4.3.4 NFRs Ontology Implementation

We used Protégé 3.3 [PROTÉGÉ] and its OWL plug-in in NFRs Ontology development.

4.4 Development of Common NFRs Terminology

There are many resources for setting up a glossary for NFRs. In addition, there are many different perspectives (see Figure 4-3) from where NFR terms are defined, (e.g. NFRs in product-oriented perspective vs. process-oriented perspective). There are few attempts to set up a common terminology for NFRs.

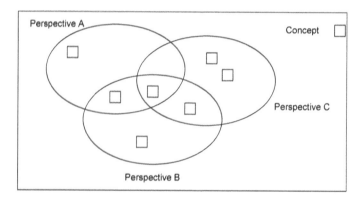

Figure 4-3: Common Terminology Derived from Different Perspectives.

In this work, the NFRs glossary is developed based on commonality analysis and generalization from the previous publications in the requirements engineering and software engineering communities. The link to the sources of the definition will be provided each time a term is defined.

Commonality analysis is a well-known technique in domain engineering (e.g. Czarnecki et al. 2000 [CE00]). A common glossary collects common terms and generalizes the definition such that the general definition could be used in the specific context.

4.4.1 Initial terms

We selected an initial set of core terms for the common NFR glossary. In order to improve the readability of this chapter, we chose to define other terms while describing the conceptual model. The initial set of core terms is the following:

- Requirement:

Although there have been many definitions used through the years, we have found the definition provided by requirements engineering authors Thayer and Dorfman [TD90] to be quite workable:

- A software capability needed by the user to solve a problem that will achieve an objective, or
- A software capability that must be met or possessed by a system or system component to satisfy a contract, standard, specification or other formally imposed documentation.

- Functional Requirement (FR):

FR is defined in [IEEE83098] as the requirement which defines the fundamental actions that must take place between the software and the environment in accepting and processing the inputs from the environment and in processing and generating the outputs to the environment. These are generally listed as shall statements starting with "The system shall..."

- Primary Functional Requirement (PFR):

PFRs are FRs which represent the principal functionalities of the system. Those are demands that require functions which directly contribute to the goal of the system, or yield direct value to its users. The identification of primary requirements (which ones to select) is similar to determining which processes in an organization are primary processes.

- Secondary Functional Requirement (SFR):

SFRs are FRs which require functionality that is secondary to the goal of the system. Examples are functions needed to manage the system or its data, logging or tracing functions, or functions that implement some legal requirement.

- Non-Functional Requirement (NFR):

Probably the greatest challenge when it comes to deal with NFRs is that there is no agreement in the literature on how to identify the term NFR in the first place. Table 4-2 gives an overview of selected definitions from the literature or the web which are representative of the definitions that exist. We provided our own definition in the last row of the table derived from experience and knowledge of the existing definitions.

Table 4-2: Definitions of the Term 'Non-Functional Requirement(s)'.

Source	Definition
Antón [Ant97]	Requirements which describe the non behavioral aspects of a system, capturing the properties and constraints under which a system must operate.
Davis [Dav93]	Requirements which represent the required overall attributes of the system, including portability, reliability, efficiency, human engineering, testability, understandability, and modifiability.
IEEE 610.12 [IEEE6101290]	Term is not defined. The standard distinguishes design requirements, implementation requirements, interface requirements, performance requirements, and physical requirements.
IEEE 830-1998 [IEEE83098]	Term is not defined. The standard defines the categories functionality, external interfaces, performance, attributes (portability, security, etc.), and design constraints. Project requirements (Such as schedule, cost, or development requirements) are explicitly excluded.
Jacobson, Booch and Rumbaugh [JBR99]	A requirement that specifies system properties, such as environmental and implementation constraints, performance, platform dependencies, maintainability, extensibility, and reliability. A requirement that specifies physical constraints on a functional requirement.
Kotonya and Sommerville [KS98]	Requirements which are not specifically concerned with the functionality of a system. They place restrictions on the product being

	developed and the development process, and they specify external constraints that the product must meet.
Mylopoulos, Chung and Nixon [MCN92]	"... global requirements on its development or operational cost, performance, reliability, maintainability, portability, robustness, and the like. (...) There is not a formal definition or a complete list of nonfunctional requirements."
Ncube [Ncu00]	The behavioral properties that the specified functions must have, such as performance, usability.
Robertson and Robertson [RR99]	A property, or quality, that the product must have, such as an appearance, or a speed or accuracy property.
SCREEN Glossary [SCREEN99]	A requirement on a service that does not have a bearing on its functionality, but describes attributes, constraints, performance considerations, design, quality of service, environmental considerations, failure and recovery.
Wiegers [Wie03]	A description of a property or characteristic that a software system must exhibit or a constraint that it must respect, other than an observable system behavior.
Wikipedia: Non-Functional Requirements [WIKIPEDIA-NFR]	Requirements which specify criteria that can be used to judge the operation of a system, rather than specific behaviors.
Wikipedia: Requirements Analysis [WIKIPEDIA-RA]	Requirements which impose constraints on the design or implementation (such as performance requirements, quality standards, or design constraints).
Our definition	Umbrella term to cover all those

	requirements which are not explicitly defined as functional.

4.5 NFRs Conceptual Model

The NFRs Ontology will define the (shared) meaning of a set of concepts for the NFRs domain. As said earlier, this can be used to improve communication and interaction among people, or even among systems. The ontology has an important core about NFRs model, but also addresses areas such as requirements, software architectures, etc.

The NFRs Ontology contains many concepts. The high-level taxonomy with the concepts is shown in Figure 4-4. In order to cope with the complexity of the model we use views of the model. A view is a model which is completely derived from another model (the base model). A view cannot be modified separately from the model from which it is derived. Changes to the base model cause corresponding changes to the view [LDS05]. Three views of the NFRs Ontology are identified: The first view concerns the NFRs relation with the other entities of the software system being developed (intermodel dependency). The second view contains the classes and properties intended to structure NFRs in terms of mutually dependent entities on other NFRs and refinements (intramodel dependency). The third view represents the measurement process and contains the concepts used to produce measures to measurable NFRs.

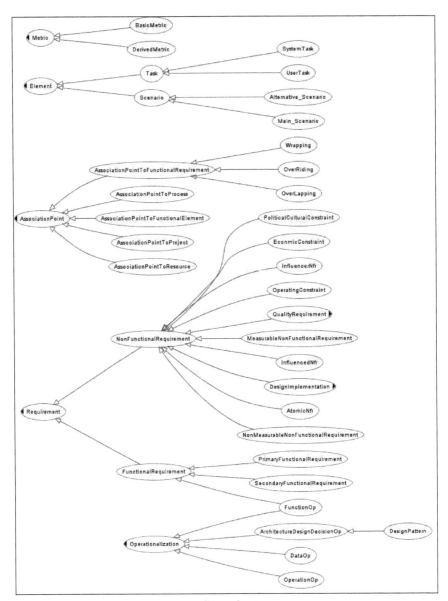

Figure: 4-4: High-Level NFRs Taxonomy.

4.5.1 Intermodel Dependency View

Figure 4-5 illustrates the structure of the NFRs intermodel dependency view by means of a simplified UML class diagram. The core of this structure relies on the fact that NFRs are not stand-alone goals, as their existence is always dependent on other concepts in the project context. If a requirement is a member of the class *NonFunctionalRequirement*, it is *necessary* for it to be a member of the class *requirement* and it is *necessary* for it to be a member of the anonymous class of things that are linked to at least one member of the class *AssociationPoint* through the *hasAssociationPoint* property. On the other hand, *isAssociatingNfrTo* links the *AssociationPoint* to a range of: *FunctionalRequirement* union *Element* union *Process* union *Product* union *Resource*. The elements of this range are described in sections 4.5.1.1, 4.5.1.2, 4.5.1.3 and 4.5.1.4.

The *AssociationPoint* can be thought of as an interface from the perspective of the association to the individuals from the above range. Thus, an individual of *AssociationPoint* class will always associate one or more NFRs to the same one individual from the above range. More specifically:

If an individual is a member of the *AssociationPoint* Class, it is necessary for it to be linked to one and only one individual from: the (*FunctionalRequirement* class through the *isAssociatingNfrTo* property) OR (*Element* through *isAssociatingNfrTo* property) OR (*Process* through *isAssociatingNfrTo* property) OR (*Product* through *isAssociatingNfrTo* property) OR (*Resource* though the *isAssociatingNfrTo* property).

An individual from *AssociationPoint* class can be linked to many individuals from the *NonFunctionalRequirement* class through *hasAssociationPoint* property.

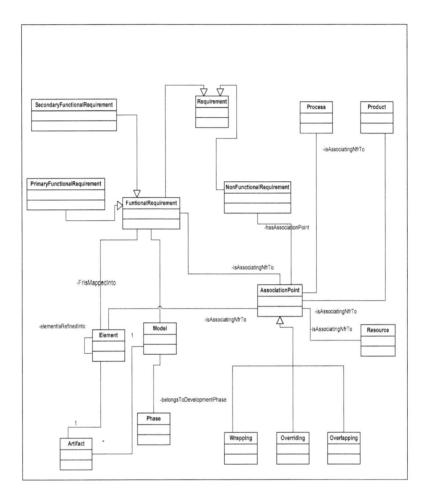

Figure: 4-5: NFRs Intermodel Dependency View.

4.5.1.1 Association to FR (or derived elements)

Functionality-related NFRs refer to the individuals instantiated from the *NonFunctionalRequirement* class and participate in *hasAssociationPoint* property to an individual from the *AssociationPoint* class which in its turn participates in *isAssociatingNfrTo* property to individual from the *FunctionalRequirement* class (see Figure 4-5). In fact, a subset of NFRs, namely functionality quality requirements (see section 4.5.2.1.1), is defined with an existential restriction to have at least one association point with FR as it represents a set of attributes that bear on the existence of a set of functions and their properties specified according to the ISO 9126 definition to the functionality quality [ISO912601]. Valid example of functionality-related NFRs is: "the interaction between the user and the software system while reading email messages must be secured".

The *FunctionalRequirement* class is further specialized into *PrimaryFunctionalRequirement* and *SecondaryFunctionalRequirement* (see Figure 4-5). A NFR can be associated to either type of FRs.

FR is further realized through the various phases of development by many functional *models* (e.g. in the object-oriented field, a use-case model is used in the requirements analysis and specification phase, a design class model is used in the software design phase, etc.). Each *model* is an aggregation of one or more *artifacts* (e.g. a use-case diagram and a use-case for the use-case model, a domain model diagram and a system sequence diagram for the analysis model, a class diagram and a communication diagram for the design model). The *artifact* by itself is an aggregation of *elements* (e.g. a class, an association, an inheritance, etc. for the class diagram). Modeling artifacts and their elements in this way gives us the option of decoupling the task of tracing NFRs from a specific development practice or paradigm.

If an NFR is associated with functionality, then some or all the offspring elements that refine this functionality will inherit this association. More specifically:

$((\mathbf{NFR_i}\ isAssociatedTo\ \mathbf{AssociationPoint_j})\ \wedge\ (\mathbf{AssociationPoint_j}\ isAssociatingNfrTo\ \mathbf{FunctionalRequirement_k})) ==> \exists\ \mathbf{Element_n}\ ((\mathbf{NFR_i}\ isAssociatedTo\ \mathbf{AssociationPoint_m})\ \wedge\ (\mathbf{AssociationPoint_m}\ isAssociatingNfrTo\ \mathbf{Element_n})\ \wedge\ (\mathbf{FunctionalRequirement_k}\ FrIsMappedInto\ \mathbf{Element_n}))$

When *hasAssociationPoint* property links an individual NFR to an individual *AssociationPoint* which is further linked to an individual *FunctionalRequirement* or *Element* through *isAsscoatingNfrTo* property, then the *AssociationPoint* can be further specified through one of three subclasses. These subclasses specify the type of association between an individual from the

NonFunctionalRequirement class and an individual from the *FunctionalRequirement* and *Element* classes. We adopt the concepts of *overlapping, overriding* and *wrapping*, commonly used in various separations of concerns approaches [RMA03] and [MAB02], to define these three subclasses:

• *Overlapping*: the NFR requirements modify the FRs they transverse. In this case, the NFR may be required before the functional ones, or it may be required after them. For example, the implementation of security requirement (e.g. user's authorization) needs to be executed *before* the user can access "read email messages" functionality.

• *Overriding*: the NFR superposes the FRs they transverse. In this case, the behavior described by the NFRs substitutes the FRs behavior.

• *Wrapping*: NFR "encapsulates" the FRs they transverse. In this case, the behavior described by the FRs is wrapped by the behavior described by the NFRs.

4.5.1.2 Association to process

A software development process is a structure imposed on the development of a software product. Synonyms include software life cycle and software process. There are several models for such processes, each describing approaches to a variety of tasks or activities that take place during the process.

From the above definition to the software process, process-related NFRs specify concerns relative to the scope of the development process. Examples of such NFRs are "The project will follow the Rational Unified Process (RUP)" and "Activities X, Y, Z will be skipped for this project".

4.5.1.3 Association to product

Product-related NFRs refer to those NFRs which have a global impact on the system as whole. Example of such NFRs are: "The system should be easy to maintain".

4.5.1.4 Association to resource

Resources serve as input to the processes used on a project. They include people, tools, materials, methods, time, money, and skills [Whi97]. An example of an NFR associated with a resource is illustrated through a requirement like "The software maintainers should have at least 2 years of experience in Oracle database." This is an operating constraint that is associated with candidates for the maintenance position for the system (another type of resources).

4.5.2 Intramodel dependency view

The intramodel dependency view is concerned with the refinement of NFRs into one or more offspring; through either *decomposition* or *operationalization*, and the correlation among the concepts of the NFRs model. The view is depicted in the UML class diagram in Figure 4-6 and it is discussed through the concepts and properties referring to: *NFRs type*, NFRs *decomposition*, NFRs *operationalization* and NFRs *interactivity*.

4.5.2.1 NFRs type

Specifying NFR into types is a particular kind of refinement for NFRs [CNYM00]. This allows for the refinement of a parent on its type on terms of offspring, each with a subtype of the parent type. Each subtype can be viewed as representing special cases for the NFR. Five subclasses are identified as a candidate for the root node for an NFR type refinement hierarchy; namely, *QualityRequirement, DesignImplementation, EconomicConstraint, OperatingConstraint* and *PoliticalCulturalConstraint*.

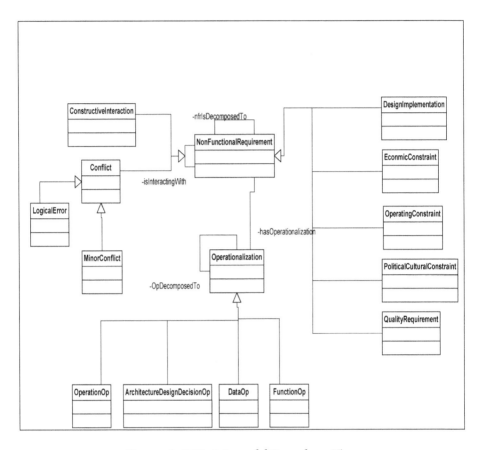

Figure 4-6: NFRs Intramodel Dependency View.

4.5.2.1.1 Quality Requirements

Quality is the totality of characteristics of an entity that bear on its ability to satisfy stated and implied needs [ISO912601]. Software Quality is an essential and distinguishing attribute of the final product. Evaluation of software products in order to satisfy software quality needs is one of the processes in the software development lifecycle. Software product quality can be evaluated by measuring internal attributes (typically static measures of intermediate products which specify internal quality from the internal view of the product), or by measuring external attributes (typically by measuring the behavior of the code when executed to specify the required level of quality from the external view), or by measuring quality in use attributes (which represents the user's view of the quality of the software product when it is used in a specific environment and a specific context of use). Figure 4-7 presents the three views of the product quality at different stages in the software life cycle.

Many approaches [BBL76], [CNYM00] and [ISO912601] classify software quality in a structured set of characteristics which are further decomposed into subcharacteristics. We built quality taxonomy out of many inputted approaches starting from the ISO 9126-1 (see Section 4.7) to define the root nodes for the quality taxonomy (External Quality, Internal Quality and Quality in Use). Figure 4-8 shows the graphical representation of the quality taxonomy, and Table A-1 (Appendix A) lists each quality with its definition against its parent quality according to the listed reference(s).

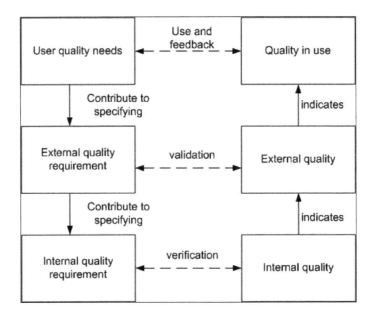

Figure: 4-7 Quality in the Software Life Cycle [ISO912601].

In the NFRs Ontology, we let the reasoner help computing condensed quality taxonomy out of the inputted proposals. Being able to use a reasoner to automatically compute the class hierarchy is one of the major benefits of building an ontology using OWL-DL sub-language. When constructing large ontologies the use of a reasoner to compute subclass-superclass relationships between classes become almost vital. Without a reasoner it is very difficult to keep large ontologies in a maintainable and logically correct state.

Figure 4-9 shows the difference between the asserted model for accuracy; the model before the reasoner impact, and the inferred model for accuracy; the model after the reasoner impact.

For example, in the asserted model, *Accuracy* is defined to be a subclass of *Integrity* according to [CNYM00], a subclass of *Reliability* according to [BBL76], a subclass of *FunctionalityQualityRequirement* according to [ISO912601] and a subclass of *Correctness* according to [Fir03]. On the other hand, in the inferred model, the reasoner has removed *FunctionalityQualityRequirement* and *Reliability* as a direct parent classes for *accuracy*. That is because Integrity is defined itself as sublass of Security according to [CNYM00] which is by itself a subclass of FunctionalityQualityRequirement. In addition, Integrity is defined as a subclass of Reliability according to [BBL76]. Thus, being a subclass of Integrity implies being a subclass of both FunctionalityQualityRequirement and Reliability classes. The reasoner simplifies the taxonomy by removing these two redundant explicit links. Similarly; for *Completeness* and *Consistency* it removed *Reliability* as a direct parent class; for *Accessibility* and *Operability* it removed Utility as a direct parent class; for *Availability* it removed *Dependability* as a direct parent class; in addition, for *Space* and *TimeBehavior*, it removed *Efficiency* as a direct parent class.

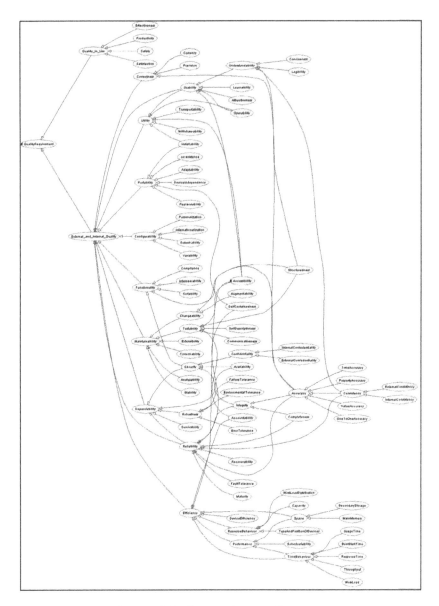

Figure: 4-8 Quality Requirements Taxonomy.

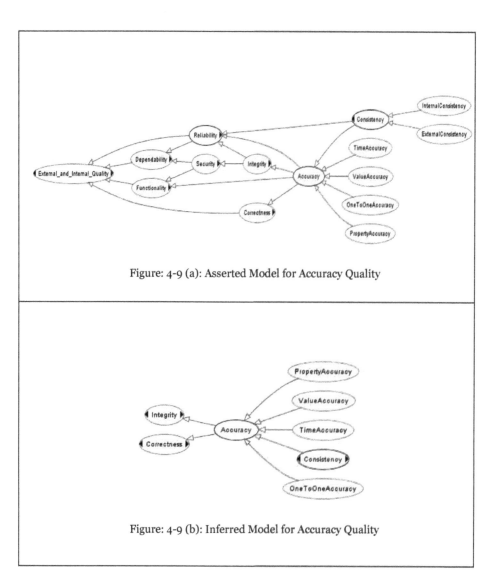

Figure: 4-9 (a): Asserted Model for Accuracy Quality

Figure: 4-9 (b): Inferred Model for Accuracy Quality

4.5.2.1.2 Design Implementation Constraint

Constraints are not subject of negotiations and, unlike qualities, are off-limits during design trade-offs. Constraints are defined in [LW03] as restrictions on the design of the system, or the process by which a system is developed, that do not affect the external behavior of the system but that must be fulfilled to meet technical, business, or contractual obligations. A key property of a constraint is that a penalty or loss of some kind applies if the constraint is not respected. According to [TEMPLATE09], the constraints on design and the implementation are being decomposed as shown in the taxonomy of Figure 4-10.

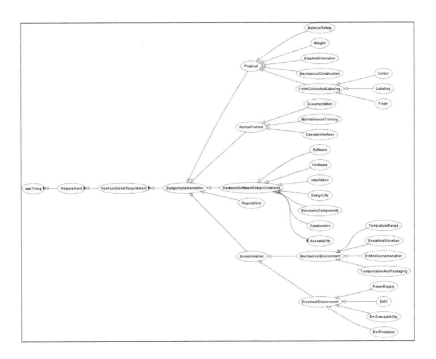

Figure 4-10: Design/Implementation Taxonomy.

4.5.2.1.3 Economic Constraint

These are constraints which include the immediate and/or long-term development cost.

4.5.2.1.4 Operating Constraint

These are constraints which include physical constraints, personnel availability, skill-level considerations, system accessibility for maintenance, etc.

4.5.2.1.5 Political / Cultural Constraint

These are constraints which include policy and legal issues (e.g. what laws and standards apply to the product).

4.5.2.2 Decomposition

This refers to the *NfrIsDecomposedTo* property that decomposes a high-level NFR into more specific sub-NFRs. In each decomposition, the offspring NFRs can contribute partially or fully towards satisficing the parent. *NfrIsDecomposedTo* is a transitive property. The decomposition can be carried either across the type dimension (section 4.5.2.1) or the association point dimension. For example, let us consider the requirement "read an email message with high security". The security requirement constitutes quite a broad topic [CNYM00]. To deal effectively with such a requirement, the NFR may need to be broken down into smaller components using the knowledge of the NFR type; discussed in Section 4.5.2.1.1, so that an effective solution can be found. Thus, the requirement stated as "read an email with a high security" can be decomposed into "read an email with high integrity", "read an email with high confidentiality", and "read an email with high availability". An example of decomposition across the Association Point is: "read inbox folder messages with high security", "read system-created folder messages with high security". The decomposition can be "ANed" (all NFR offspring are required to achieve the parent NFR goal) or "ORed" (it is sufficient that one of the offspring be achieved instead, the choice of offspring being guided by the stakeholders) [CNYM00].

In the case of "ANed", as in the *security* example, all the sub-NFRs are also associated with the Association Point with which the parent NFR is associated. For example, the set of individuals of *AssociationPoint* class which participates in *hasAssociationPoint* property with *security* is a subset of the set of individuals of *AssociationPoint* class which participate in *hasAssociationPoint* property with *confidentiality, integrity,* or *availability*. In the case of "ORed", then only the sub-NFRs that are selected by stakeholders will be associated with the FRs with which the parent NFR is associated. Figures 4-11-a and 4-11-b illustrate the two situations. The question mark notation "?" in (3-11-b) indicates that a further contribution from the stakeholders is required to determine the existence of the relation.

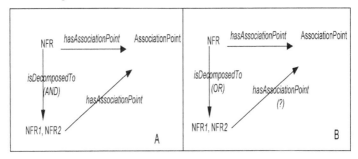

Figure: 4-11: Implicit Relations among NFRs and Association Points.

NFRs which cannot be further decomposed into sub-NFRs are referred to as Atomic NFRs. That is if an individual is a member of class AtomicNfr, then it cannot participate in NfrIsDecomposedTo relation as a domain element.

4.5.2.3 Operationalization

This refers to the *hasOperationalization* property that refines the NFR into solutions in the target system that will satisfice the NFR [CNYMoo]. The inferred taxonomy of the operationalization is presented in Figure 4-12 and it shows that operationalization corresponds to solutions that provide operations, functions (*FunctionOp*), data representations and architecture design decisions (e.g. design pattern) in the target system to meet the needs stated in the NFRs. Similar to decomposition, operationalization can be ANed or ORed.

In the inferred model, the reasoner classifies *FunctionOp* based on the imposed assertions as a subclass for *FunctionalRequirement*. This classification is consistent with many arguments in the requirements engineering community on the tight link between the FRs and NFRs [PDKVo2]. The ontology brings formalism and a concrete understanding to this link.

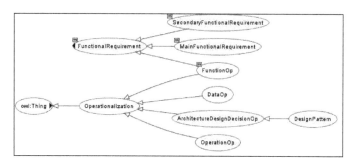

Figure: 4-12: Inferred Taxonomy for Operationalizations.

We note, that the existence of an association between a NFR and an association point (e.g. *security* and association point for *send email*) implies that an association exists between those operationalizations which are derived from the NFR and that association point (e.g. the use of additional ID and association point for send email). Figure 4-13 illustrates this relationship.

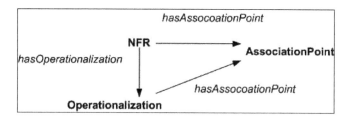

Figure 4-13: Implicit Relations among NFRs, Operationalizations and AssociationPoints.

4.5.2.4 Interactivity

An individual NFR may participate in *isInteractingWith* property which links it to another NFR. This refers to the fact that the achievement of one NFR; *InfluencerNfr*, at a certain association point can hinder (through *isNegativelyInteractingWith* property) or help (through *isPositivelyInteractingWith* property) the achievement of other NFR; *InfluencedNfr*, at the same association point, e.g. *security* and *performance* at *read an email message* functionality. *isInteractingWith* is not a symmetric property.

If NFR$_1$ participates in the relation *isNegativelyInteractingWith* with NFR$_2$, then we say that there is a conflict between NFR$_1$ and NFR$_2$. A conflict among two or more NFRs occurs when the achievement of one NFR obstructs the achievement of another.

The negative interaction is further specialized through the two sub-properties, which help classifying the negative interaction into: *hasLogicalErrorWith* and *hasMinorContradictionWith*. We chose to focus on these two sources of conflict because they are general enough to identify the most critical conflicts (logical errors) with which the developers have to deal first, and to allow a flexible quantification of the level of criticality of the remaining conflicts for further consideration (Contradiction).

Logical Error: This is a fundamental conflict which must be resolved immediately. It occurs when the achievement of NFR$_1$ will prevent the achievement of NFR$_2$. This is expressed by means of the proposition LogicalError (NFR$_1$, NFR$_2$) $\Leftrightarrow$ NFR$_1$ $\rightarrow$ NOT NFR$_2$. Logical Error demonstrates a direct contradiction between two requirements. For example, NFR$_1$ is stated as "Security has to be high at *read email* functionality"; while NFR$_2$ is stated as "There should be no security constraints at *read email* functionality"!

Minor Contradiction: This is one of the best-known cases of conflict [CNYMoo]. Here, we emphasize that NFRs by themselves do not interact, as they represent static goals to be achieved. However, their associations with association points could interact, in that attempts to achieve one NFR at a certain association point can hinder (negative interaction) or help (positive interaction) the achievement of other NFRs at the same association point. Associating a win condition with an NFR (say NFR$_1$) triggers a search of the operationalization that has positive and/or negative effects on NFR$_1$. For example, the Portability NFR, the win condition of which is "portable to Windows", has positive effects on the portability layers and separation of data generation and on the presentation, but has negative effects on the use of fast platform-dependent user interface functionalities that would be affected with the layering strategy. The operationalizations that are found to have negative effects on other NFRs sharing the same association points with their parents NFRs are used to identify potential conflicts. Below is a generalized algorithm for NFR conflict identification:

Algorithm: Quality_Conflict_Identification(ASSOCIATION_POINTx)

// Find an NFR which links to the same association point. And Initialize CONFLICT.
Find NFRx such that return_associated_NFR(ASSOCIATION_POINTx)
CONFLICT ← Φ

// Get Positive OPerationalizations (POP) and negative OPerationalizations (NOP)
For each NFRx in return_associated_NFR(ASSOCIATION_POINTx)

begin
POP ← {OPi | positively-influences (OPi, NFRx) AND parent_NFR(OPi) ∈ return_associated_NFR(ASSOCIATION_POINTx)}
NOP ← {OPi | negatively-influences (OPi, NFRx) AND parent_NFR(OPi) ∈ return_associated_NFR(ASSOCIATION_POINTx)}

// Identify conflicts using positive-negative or negative-positive relationships.
For each OPi in POP
CONFLICT ← CONFLICT ∪
{(ASSx, ASSy) | negatively-influences (OPi, NFRy) AND (NFRy ∈ return_associated_NFR(ASSOCIATION_POINTx))}

For each OPi in NOP
CONFLICT ← CONFLICT ∪
{(ASSx, ASSy) | positively-influences (OPi, NFRy) AND (NFRy ∈ return_associated_NFR(ASSOCIATION_POINTx))}
End for;

Table 4-3 shows a summary of what we collected through our observations of industry and the literature of some NFRs, including some of their popular operationalizations, and other top-NFRs which are candidates for establishing a conflict involving a minor-contradiction. We make the note, however, that Table 4-3 does not pretend to be complete. Indeed, it can not be complete as new experiences by the authors and also by other researchers on NFRs can add new insights into understanding the minor contradictions among NFRs.

Table 4-3: NFR operationalizations and Candidate Minor Contradictions.

PRIMARY NFR	OPERATIONALIZATIONS	OTHER NFR CONFLICTS
Usability	Error-reducing user input/output	Effort Performance
	Input acceptability checking	Effort Performance
Reusability	Domain architecture-driven	Effort Performance
	Layering	Effort Performance
Security	Authorization	Availability Multi-Access Effort Performance
	Request additional ID	Usability Effort Performance
Space	Use compressed format	Response time Effort
Response time	Use indexing	Effort
Interoperability	Input acceptability checking	Effort Performance
	Layering	Effort Performance
Dependability	Backup/ recovery	Evolvability Effort Performance
	Monitoring & Control	Effort Availability Performance Multi-access
Evolvability	Layering	Effort Performance

Figure 4-14 depicts the two types of conflict that may arise between two NFRs.

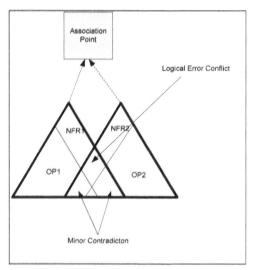

Figure: 4-14: Conflicts Between Two NFRs

4.5.3 NFRs Measurement View

This view refers to the classes and properties which represent measurement model concepts associated with the class *MeasurableNonFunctionalRequirement*. Figure 4-15 shows the relationships among the key components of the measurement model: *MeasurableNonFunctionalRequirement*, *Indicator*, *BaseMeasures* and *DerivedMeasures* by means of a simplified UML class diagram.

For an individual to be a member of *MeasurableNonFunctionalRequirement* class, it has to be a member of *NonFunctionalRequirement* class and it is necessary for it to be a member of the anonymous class of things that are linked to at least one member of the class *QualityIndicator* through the *hasIndicator* property. A measurement planner defines measurement indicators that link the NFRs to a specified information need.

The measurement model linked to a *MeasurableNonFunctionalRequirement* captures the process of quantifying and interpreting the measurement data needed for decision making. An indicator is a measure that provides an estimate or evaluation of specified attributes derived from the analysis of the measurement data (values) with respect to defined *decision criteria*, which serves as basis for decision-making by the measurement users. For example, acceptable range of software reliability values is [75%, 100%]; and values below 75% would require more testing of the product until an acceptable level is reached. *Indicator* class is linked to the class *Measure* through *hasMeasure* property.

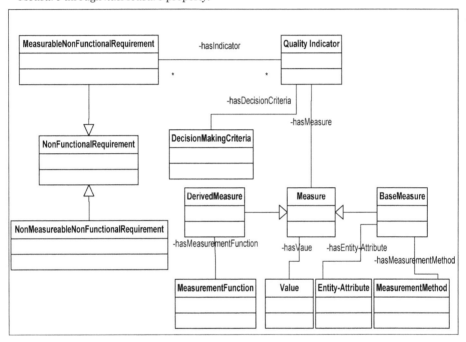

Figure: 4-15: NFR Measurement View

A measure is a variable to which a value is assigned. It can be a base measure or derived measure. A base measure is defined in terms of an *Entity-Attribute* and a *MeasurementMethod* which is a logical sequence of operations with the purpose of quantifying an attribute of software entity. An example of such base measures are: lines of code (LOC), or Kemerer and Chidamber suite [CK94] that have been defined for the object oriented programming. A derived measure is a measure that is defined as a function of two or more base measures. It is quantified by a *MeasurementFunction* - an algorithm or calculation performed to combine two or more base measures. For instance one can decide that the measure of maintainability is obtained by a formula like: αAnalysability + βChangeability + γStability + δTestability, where the weights α, β, γ, δ are obtained by a statistical analysis process [ISO912601].

The NFRs measurement view is compatible with the ISO/IEC standard 15939 [ISO1593907] and the described there measurement information model which is defined as a structure linking measurement information needs to the relevant entities and attributes of concern.

4.6 Evaluation

This chapter described, through an ontology, glossaries and taxonomies for NFRs. We used these glossaries for generalization to the common NFRs concepts. The ontology is a first version meant to evolve. This book does not claim that NFRs Ontology is a complete ontology. The book aims to consolidate core and support knowledge about NFRs into a practical, workable and, most importantly, extensible NFRs Ontology.

These factors make NFRs Ontology useful in its current form, as well as adaptable to other new applications or concerns, even if NFRs Ontology is not complete.

The evaluation criterion for the discussed ontology is that the Common Foundation for NFRs should be (i) generally acceptable for stakeholders in requirements engineering community, (ii) consistent and (iii) accurate. 'Generally accepted' means that the knowledge and practices described are applicable to most projects most of the time, and that there is widespread consensus about their value and usefulness. 'Generally accepted' does not mean that the knowledge and practices described are or should be applied uniformly on all projects [PMBOK00].

Clearly, the evaluation of the acceptance and the accuracy of the ontology as such ultimately relies upon its application in different contexts. For the purpose of this evaluation, we have instantiated the NFRs Ontology against the set of requirements from the settings of the NOKIA Mobile Email Application System (Chapter 3, Section 3.3.1) and the IEEE Montreal Website (Chapter 3, Section 3.3.2). Further, we worked closely with an expert from SAP-Montreal to use the NFRs Ontology as a repository for the requirements of one of the projects which are under development (Chapter 3, Section 3.3.3).

Figure 4-16, shows a snapshot for the instantiated NFRs Ontology against the set of requirements from the IEEE Montreal website project. For this visualization, we used TGVizTab plug-in. Table 4-4 summarizes the total number of individuals per project instantiated from some of the core classes in the NFRs Ontology.

Table 4-4: Summary of Numbers of Individuals Instantiated of NFRs Ontology.

	NOKIA Mobile Email Application	IEEE Montreal Website	SAP Project
FunctionalRequirement	45	39	104
Element	189	223	421
NonFunctionalRequirement	18	13	21
QualityRequirement	13	8	15
DesignImplementationConstraint	2	2	3
OperatingConstraint	1	1	1
PoliticalCulturalConstraint	1	2	1
EconomicConstraint	1	0	1
Resource	N/A	7	6
AssociationPoint	17	39	27
Operationalization	34	13	24
ArchitectureDesignOp	15	6	2
DataOp	2	1	0
FunctionOp	15	6	17
OperationOp	2	0	5

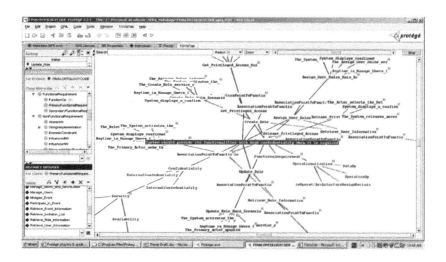

Figure 4-16: Instantiated NFRs Ontology Against IEEE Montreal Website Case Study.

From the experiences and the participants' feedback developed from instantiating the NFRs Ontology against the three real-life projects (the Nokia project, the IEEE Montreal website project and the SAP project), the ontology has proven to be easy to instantiate and links the concepts efficiently. Each individual captured NFR was instantiated from its corresponding concept in the Ontology. We make the note here that we did not meet the case in which an individual NFR was not instantiated from a corresponding concept.

In order to facilitate the adoption of the NFRs Ontology in the requirements specification phase, we further built a recommended process of steps towards instantiating the NFRs Ontology (Figure 4-17).

- **_Instantiation of the InterModel Dependency View_**:
  - – Instantiate classes: Resource, Process, Product.
  - – Instantiate class FunctionalRequirement.
  - – Instantiate classes representing the functional refinements: Model, Phase, Artifact, Element.
  - – Instantiate class NonFunctionalRequirement.
  - – Instantiate class AssociationPoint.
  - – Link individuals from AssociationPoint class to individuals from classes: FunctionalRequirement, Element, Resource, Process and Product.
  - – Link individuals from NonFunctionalRequirement class to the individuals from AssociationPoint class.
- **_Instantiation of the Intramodel Dependency View_**:
  - – Link individuals from NonFunctionalRequirement class to other individuals from NonFunctionalRequirement class through isDecomposedTo property.
  - – Instantiate class Operationalization.
  - – Link individuals from NonFunctionalRequirement class to individuals from Operationalizations through hasOperationalization property.
  - – Link individuals from Operationalization class to individuals from AssociationPoint class.
  - – Link individuals from NonFunctionalRequirement class to other individuals from NonFunctionalRequirement class through isInteractingWith property.
- **_Instantiation of Measurement View:_**
  - – Instantiate classes: MeasurableNonFuncionalRequirement, Indicator, DecisionMakingCriteria, Measure and Value.
  - – Link individuals from MeasurableNonFunctionalRequirement class to individuals from QualityIndicaor class.
  - – Link individuals from QualityIndicator class to individuals from DecisionMakingCriteria class.
  - – Link individuals from QualityIndicator class to indivifuals from Measure class.
  - – Link individuals from Measure class to individuals from Value class.

Figure 4-17: Steps Towards Instantiating NFRs Ontology.

The snapshots in Figures 4-18 and 4-19 are taken while instantiating some NFRs of the IEEE Montreal Website Project. The properties widgets in the individual editor on the right half of the screen helps to link an individual to other concepts through its allowed relations.

Further, The NFRs Ontology has demonstrated its usefulness on checking of the completeness of the requirements. For example, there is an asserted condition on the *Operationalization* concept that it has to be linked to the NonFunctionalRequirement concept through *isOperationalizationOf* relationship (inverse of *hasOperationalization* relationship). If an instance of the *Operationalization* class is created without being linked to its NFR, then the widget corresponding to *isOperationalizationOf* relation will be highlighted in red to attract the attention towards this missing link (See Figure 4-20). With such a feature, NFRs can be checked for their completeness against the asserted conditions discussed in this chapter.

Consistency has been demonstrated through the usage of a semantic web reasoning system and information repository: Renamed Abox and Concept Expression Reasoner (RACER) [RACER].

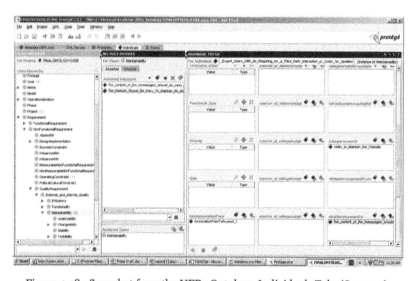

Figure 4-18: Snapshot from the NFRs Ontology-Individuals Tab- (Screen 1).

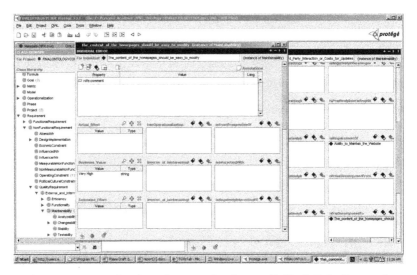

Figure 4-19: Snapshot from the NFRs Ontology-Individuals Tab- (Screen 2).

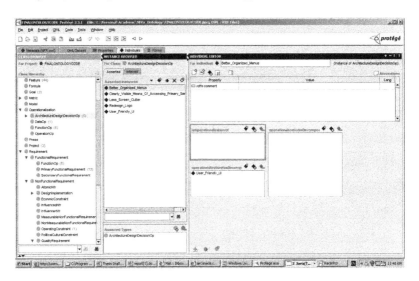

Figure 4-20: Snapshot from The NFRs Ontology-Individuals Tab- (Screen 3).

In [HM06], the authors propose a new requirements elicitation method ORE (Ontology based Requirements Elicitation), where a domain ontology can be used as domain knowledge. In their method, a domain ontology plays a role on semantic domain which gives meanings to requirements statements by using a semantic function. By using inference rules on the ontology and a quality metrics on the semantic function, an analyst can be navigated which requirements should be added for improving completeness of the current version of the requirements and/or which requirements should be deleted from the current version for keeping consistency. The method starts when an analyst maps the requirements items (statements) in a requirement document into atomic concepts of the ontology. By using this approach, it is possible to estimate the quality of requirements through four defined quality characteristics: Correctness, Completeness, Consistency and Ambiguity. Requirements engineers can benefit from the NFRs Ontology proposed in this chapter combined with the proposed method in [HM06] to evaluate the set of requirements against these four quality characteristics.

4.7 Related Work

Even though there is no formal definition of the term 'NFR', there has been considerable work on characterizing and classifying NFRs. In a report published by the Rome Air Development Center (RADC) [BWT85], NFRs ("software quality attributes" in their terminology) are classified into consumer-oriented (or software quality factors) and technically-oriented (or software quality criteria). The former class of software attributes refers to software qualities observable by the consumer, such as efficiency, correctness and interoperability. The latter class addresses system-oriented requirements such as anomaly management, completeness and functional scope.

Earlier work by Boehm et al. [BBL76] structured quality characteristics of software within a quality characteristics tree of 25 nodes, noting that merely increasing designer awareness would improve the quality of the final product. On a different track, Hauser et al. [HC88] provide a methodology for reflecting customer attributes in different phases of automobile design.

Dobson et al [DLS05] describe an approach to specifying the Quality of Service (QoS) requirements of service-centric systems using an ontology for Quality of Service. The above approaches address only a subset of NFRs; namely quality requirements, and sometimes within a specific context; (e.g. service computing in [DLS05]). On contrast, our work aims at providing a more generic solution to all types of NFRs with independence from any context.

Al Balushi and Dabhi [ASDL07] used an ontology-based approach to build NFR quality models with the objective to gather reusable requirements during NFR specification. We agree with these authors on the usefulness of ontology, however, the research objectives of their research efforts and ours differ, which in turn, leads to essential difference in the research outcomes. While the conceptual model in [ASDL07] is geared towards solving requirements reuse problems, our ontology covers a broader spectrum of NFR issues. This is achieved by using multiple views, which explicate requirements phenomena by complementing the strengths of multiple conceptualizations of NFRs.

Lee et al. [LMGYA06] apply the so-called *"method for developing a problem domain ontology"* from natural language security requirements from various sources. The objective of the research by these authors was to provide support to a common understanding of security requirements and to facilitate analysis at various decision points by making the required information readily available with appropriate context and format. While this approach is focused on security requirements, ours is meant to help analysing any NFR.

On the other hand, some standards have been proposed in order to unify the definition of subsets of NFRs; e.g. software quality concepts [ISO912601]. However, till now there is no clear and coherent generic representation of the NFRs concepts. The most important of these standards is the ISO 9126 [ISO912601]. ISO 9126 is an international standard for the evaluation of software quality. The fundamental objective of this standard is to address some of the well known human biases that can adversely affect the delivery and perception of a software development project. These biases include changing priorities after the start of a project or not having any clear definitions of "success". By clarifying, then agreeing on the project priorities and subsequently converting abstract priorities (compliance) to measurable values (output data can be validated against schema X with zero intervention), ISO 9126 tries to develop a common understanding of the project's objectives and goals.

The standard is divided into four parts:

- quality model

- external metrics

- internal metrics

- Quality in use metrics.

In [ACK05], the authors reported on nine problems with ISO/IEC 9126 for design quality as follows:

• Some concept definitions are ambiguous, e.g. *functional compliance.*

• Some concept definitions overlap, e.g. *functional implementation completeness* and *functional implementation coverage*.

• Overlapping definition of concepts can lead to multiple counting when metrics are constructed.

• The standard recognizes reliability and maintainability as quality characteristics but does not refer to them when considering design products although most software engineers would agree that both characteristics need to be designed into products.

• The standard ignores other characteristics that might be important in design products such as validity and modularity.

• Simple Counts are insufficient to evaluate the quality of design.

• Some measures require information that is not available to the designers, such as *functional understandability*.

• Some measures require counting items that are not available from design documents, such as *computational accuracy* and *data exchange*.

• No guidelines or procedures are defined for accumulating the metrics into an overall evaluation.

In the light of its ambiguities and omissions, the authors of [ACK05] conclude that ISO/IEC 9126 in its present format fails to achieve any of its stated objectives.

In 2005, the ISO/IEC 25000:2005 [ISO25000] has been introduced as a guidance for the use of the new series of International Standards named Software product Quality Requirements and Evaluation (SQuaRE).

SQuaRE replaces the current ISO/IEC 9126 [ISO912601] series and the 14598 series. SQuaRE consists of the following five divisions:

• ISO/IEC 2500n - Quality Management Division,

• ISO/IEC 2501n - Quality Model Division,

• ISO/IEC 2502n - Quality Measurement Division,

• ISO/IEC 2503n - Quality Requirements Division, and

• ISO/IEC 2504n - Quality Evaluation Division,

ISO/IEC 25050 to ISO/IEC 25099 are reserved to be used for SQuaRE extension International Standards and/or Technical Reports. SQuaRE provides:

• Terms and definitions,

• Reference models,

• General guide,

• Individual division guides, and

- International Standards for requirements specification, planning and management, measurement and evaluation purposes.

SQuaRE includes International Standards on quality model and measures, as well as on quality requirements and evaluation.

In Table 4-5, we compare different broad quality taxonomies, including our constructed quality taxonomy presented in Section 4.5.2.1.1, with respect to (i) number of qualities included, (ii) consideration to association, (iii) consideration to operationalization, (iv) consideration to interactivity among qualities and (v) consideration to qualities measure.

Table 4-5: Comparison Between Several Broad Quality Taxonomies.

Quality taxonomy proposal	Number of quality requirements	Association	Operationalization	Interactivity among Qualities	Measurement of quality requirement
[MRW77]	11	N/A	N/A	N/A	N/A
[Wie03]	12	N/A	N/A	N/A	N/A
[BWT85]	13	N/A	N/A	N/A	N/A
[BBT76]	20	N/A	N/A	N/A	N/A
[ISO912601]	37	N/A	N/A	N/A	Considered in ISO 9126 [2], ISO 9126 [3] and ISO 9126 [4]
Our Quality Taxonomy	87	Association with five potential association points is well presented in Section 4.5.1	Operationalization property is well presented in Section 4.5.2.3	Interactivity is well presented in Section 4.5.2.4	A broad measurement view that accommodates the wider range of qualities is well presented in Section 4.5.3. The view conforms to the ISO/IEC standard 15939

Chapter V: A Traceability Mechanism for Change Management of Non-Functional Requirements

"Testing by itself does not improve software quality. Test results are an indicator of quality, but in and of themselves, they don't improve it. Trying to improve software quality by increasing the amount of testing is like try to lose weight by weighing yourself more often. What you eat before you step onto the scale determines how much you will weigh, and the software development techniques you use determine how many errors testing will find. If you want to lose weight, don't buy a new scale; change your diet. If you want to improve your software, don't test more; develop better."

Steve McConnell

5.1 Introduction

In the early phases of software development, user requirements are established based on an analysis of business goals and the application domain. Subsequently, architectures of the desired systems are designed and implemented. As indicated already in the Introduction, during this development process, requirements are usually exposed to many changes as the availability of knowledge on the system being developed increases [Jac07]. Traceability, defined as "the ability to describe and follow the life of a requirement in both a forwards and backwards direction" from inception throughout the entire system's life cycle, provides useful support mechanisms for managing requirement changes during the ongoing change process [Got95] and [GF94]. Moreover, the extent to which traceability is exploited is viewed as an indicator of system quality and process maturity, and is mandated by many standards [ANRS06].

In practice, many organizations either focus their traceability efforts on FRs [WW03] or else fail entirely to implement an effective traceability process [BSA07] and [Cle05]. NFRs such as security, safety, performance, and reliability are treated in a rather ad hoc fashion and are rarely traced. Furthermore, the tendency for NFRs to have a global impact upon the software system necessitates the need to create and maintain an overwhelming number of traceability links. On the other hand, the appropriate support for NFRs traceability can return significant benefits to an organization through helping analysts understand the impact of a proposed change upon critical system qualities and enabling them to maintain these qualities throughout the lifetime of a software system.

In chapter 4, we proposed a conceptualization of NFRs which provides explicit links to concepts and relations of NFRs and thus serves as a foundation for validating the semantic precision of conceptual schemas and for mapping NFR conceptual knowledge to modern Web-enabled ontology languages such as OWL [OWL]. A knowledge-based representation; such as the one we presented in Chapter 4, is necessary to support the traceability of NFRs within a system and to provide practitioners and researchers with a valuable alternative to current requirements engineering techniques.

In this chapter, we identify four critical areas in which NFRs require traceability support:

- Impact of changes to FRs on NFRs (inter-model traceability).
- Impact of changes to NFRs on FRs (inter-model traceability).
- Impact of changes to NFRs on sub-NFRs and parent NFRs (intra-model traceability).
- Impact of changes to NFRs on other interacting NFRs (intra-model traceability).

Tracing NFRs against these areas is crucial to the long-term maintenance of critical system qualities such as safety, security, reliability, usability, and performance.

In this chapter we provide a traceability mechanism using Datalog expressions [UW02] to implement queries on the relational model-based representation for the ontology. Datalog (a subset of Prolog) is a language of facts and rules, as well as a logic-based query language for the relational model. Query evaluation with Datalog is sound and complete. In addition, Datalog supports Recursive Closure Operations which makes it possible to trace through multiple levels of refinements within the software development process. Furthermore, Semantic Web Rule Language (SWRL) which is a proposal for a Semantic Web rules-language is combining sublanguages of the OWL Web Ontology Language (OWL DL and Lite) with those of the Rule Markup Language (Unary/Binary Datalog). SWRL allows users to write rules that can be expressed in terms of OWL concepts to provide more powerful deductive reasoning capabilities than OWL alone [SWRL]. Semantically, SWRL is built on the same description logic foundation as OWL and provides similar strong formal guarantees when performing inference.

This brings a feasible future work towards using our Datalog implementation proposed in this chapter to extend our OWL implementation for NFRs Ontology through the definition of SWRL rules.

In addition to Datalog implementation, we provide an alternative implementation using the eXtensible Markup Language (XML)-based representation. We then use XQuery [XQUERY] to implement queries to represent requirements tracing information. XQuery, which is a technology under development by the W3C, provides the means to extract and manipulate data from XML documents or any data source that can be captured in XML, such as relational databases or office documents. XQuery uses XPath expression syntax to address specific parts of an XML document.

The remainder of this chapter is organized as follows: Section 5.2 provides a brief overview of related work. Section 5.3 presents the relational model and implementation of tracing queries using Datalog expressions. Section 5.4 presents an alternative implementation using XML and XQuery expressions. Section 5.5 proposes a traceability mechanism using the NFRs Ontology and the relational model. Section 5.6 provides a discussion and evaluation and Section 5.7 concludes the chapter.

5.2 Related work

Although prior work on tracing NFRs has been rather limited, a number of traceability approaches have in fact been developed to support related activities while incorporating NFRs in software engineering processes.

In [CNY95], the authors adopt the NFR Framework [CNYM00] to show how a historical record of the treatment of NFRs during the development process can also serve to systematically support evolution of the software system. The authors treat changes in terms of (i) adding or modifying NFRs, or changing their relative importance, and (ii) changing design decisions or design rationale. While this study has provided some support for extensions to the NFR Framework, particularly in representing changes to goal achievement strengths, the impact of changes to functional models on non-functional models, and vice-versa, has yet to be discussed.

In [Cle05] and [CSBBC05], the authors propose an approach named Goal Centric Traceability, a holistic traceability environment which provides systems analysts with the means to manage the impact of functional change on NFRs. Nevertheless, the impact of changes to an NFR on other NFRs and the functional model is not solved with this solution.

Many other initial approaches have been introduced by researchers active in the requirements engineering, product line engineering, and Aspect oriented Software Engineering communities to address the traceability of NFRs [EG04], [FE00], [Sam06], [RJ01], [HNS05], [Jac07], [BCAMRT06], [NI07], [ANRS06], [GF94], [Let02] and [WSZA06]. These approaches have three important limitations. First, tracing is either tackled within a phase or it does not cover the entire life cycle. Second, the traceability model that is applied is usually focused on specific programming paradigm elements. Third, these approaches use coarse-grained entities for tracing purposes, which is risky from the point of view of the precision of change impact analysis, which in turn results in imprecise estimates of the cost and time involved in implementing a requirement change. The specific challenges faced in state-of-the art traceability practice are described in more detail in [ANRS06].

This chapter offers a solution to the open research problems discussed in this section. The proposed ontology in Chapter 4 is well suited for defining and analyzing numerous NFRs, the impact of changes in a NFR upon other NFRs, NFRs impact on the FRs and vice versa traceable over the entire life cycle.

5.3 Relational data model for tracing requirements

While the metamodels presented to describe the ontology in Chapter 4, Figures 4-5, 4-6 and 4-15 are useful ways to understand the abstract structure of the NFRs-related concepts, they are not considered a suitable basis for retrieving data on the objects that are instantiated from this model. Thus, the model has to be transformed into another model which facilitates querying the information. The relational model is extremely useful as a mapping vehicle, because it is based on a single data modeling concept, namely the relation. For the purposes of this work, we decided to use Datalog expressions [UW02] to operate on one or more relations to yield another relation which would present the desired results. Figure 5-1 presents the schemas for the relations corresponding to the subset of concepts shown in Figures 4-5 and 4-6. The relations are intended to hold information collected by stakeholders at different stages of the development cycle.

To illustrate the traceability model, we will limit the discussion to two pieces of functionality of NOKIA Mobile Email application (see Chapter 3, Section 3.1): (1) the user asks to read an email message; and (2) the user composes and sends a new email. Figure 5-2 presents these two main pieces of functionality decomposed into elements of use cases, scenarios, events, and methods. The decomposition of FRs into these elements is for illustrative purposes. Our traceability approach would also support mapping FRs into other refinement elements (e.g. elements of the static view of the system such as classes and relations).

Three NFRs are also presented: security, performance, and scalability.

```
//Schema refers to  NonFunctionalRequirement concept
NFR (ID, NAME, DESCRIPTION, SATISFACTION, TYPE);
//Schema refers to  FunctionalRequirement concept
FR (ID, NAME, DESCRIPTION);
//Schema refers to  operationalization concept
OP (OP_ID, NAME, DESCRIPTION);
//Scheme refers to  nfrIsDecomposedTo relation
NFR_DECOMPOSITION (DEC_ID, PARENT_NFR_ID, SUB_NFR_ID, TYPE_OF_DECOMPOSITION);
//scheme refers to hasOperationalization relation (from the NFR to the design solutions)
NFR_OP (NFR_ID, OP_ID);
//Schema refers to OpDecomposedTo relation
OP_DECOMPOSITION (OP_DEC_ID, PARENT_OP_ID, SUB_OP_ID, TYPE_OF_DECOMPOSITION);
//Schema refers to isInteractingWith relation
NFR_INTERACTION (INTERACTION_ID, INTERACTING_ASSOCIATION_ID, AFFECTED_ASSOCIATION_ID,
TYPE_OF_INTERACTION);
//Schema refers to hasAssociationPoint relation
NFR_ASSOCIATION (ASSOCIATION_ID, NFR_ID, ASSOCIATION_POINT_ID, Type);
//Schema refers to FRisMappedInto relation
FR_ELEMENT (FR_ID, ELEMENT_ID);
//Schema refers to elementIsDecomposedInto relation
ELEMENT_DECOMPOSITION (PARENT_ELEMENT_ID, CHILD_ELEMENT_ID);
```

Figure 5-1: Schematic representation of some concepts and relations presented in Figures 4-5
and 4-6.

While populating the relations, it is hard to ensure the completeness of the information, as the
majority of the instances of the relations are not directly stated by stakeholders, but they hold as
valid relations by induction. For example, *security* could be known as being participating in
hasAssociationPoint relation with individual from *AssociationPoint* class which in its turn
participates in *isAssociatingNfrTo* relation with the individual *"read an email message"*
instantiated from *FunctionalRequirement* class. *Confidentiality*, which is derived from *security*
by "ANed" decomposition (through *NfrIsDecomposedTo* relation), also participates in
hasAssociationPoint relation with the same individual from *AssociationPoint* class which
participates in its turn in *isAssociatingNfrTo* relation with *"read an email message"* according
to Figure 4-11. This information on *confidentiality* association could be missed when populating
the NFR_ASSOCIATION relation, yet this relation has to be traced on possible related requested
changes in requirements. Our tracing mechanism considers this situation, and is implemented
so that it provides the suitable solution.

We identify four critical areas in which NFRs require traceability support. These areas are discussed in the following subsections.

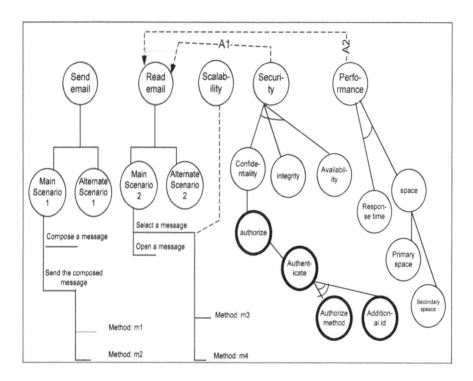

Figure 5-2: Illustration of FR and NFR Relations through the Email System.

5.3.1 Impact of Changes to Functional Models on NFRs

When a change is initiated in an FR, the set of NFRs potentially affected needs to be identified and retrieved. This is accomplished by first retrieving all the directly associated NFRs from the relation NFR_ASSOCIATION. In order to ensure the completeness of the trace and the consistency among requirements, it is important that all NFRs associated with all elements derived from the affected FR against the requested change be analyzed as well. This should be done in a recursive manner to cover all possible derived elements. The following Datalog expressions implement this query:

// R_TEMP refers to a temporary relation.

/* FR_CHANGED and NFR_CHANGED refer to the ID of the FR and the NFR, the 'request changes' from which the need for traceability was triggered. */

/* RESULT refers to the desired relation that holds the data result. */

R1_TEMP(Y) ← FR_ELEMENT(X,Y) , X = "FR_CHANGED"

R2_TEMP (Q, W) ← ELEMENT_DECOMPOSITION (Q, W), R1_TEMP (Y), Q = Y

R2_TEMP (Q, W) ← ELEMENT_DECOMPOSITION (Q, Z) , R2_TEMP (Z, W)

RESULT (B) ← NFR_ASSOCIATION (A, B, C, D) , C = "FR_CHANGED"

RESULT(B) ← NFR_ASSOCIATION (A, B, C, D), R2_TEMP (Q, W), C= Q

RESULT(B) ← NFR_ASSOCIATION (A, B, C, D), R2_TEMP (Q, W), C= W

It is important to note that the decomposition of NFRs will never have a circular dependency. This is a necessary condition for the termination of R2_TEMP. In the case study of the mobile email system (see Figure 5-2), if a change is requested to the *read an email message* functionality, then the above query expressions will retrieve *security, performance,* and *scalability* as potentially impacted NFRs.

5.3.2 Impact of Changes to Nonfunctional Models on Functional Models

To ensure a complete inter-model traceability, we should consider the impact of changes to NFRs on the functional model to complement the query in Section 5.3.1 which considered the impact of changes of functional models to NFRs. When a change is initiated in an NFR, then the set of all association points of the FR type or of the element type should be retrieved and analyzed against the potential change. The following Datalog expressions implement this query:

RESULT(B) ← NFR_ASSOCIATION (A, B, C, D), D = "FR", B = "NFR_CHANGED".

RESULT(B) ← NFR_ASSOCIATION (A, B, C, D), D = "ELEMENT", B = "NFR_CHANGED".

In the mobile email system (see Figure 5-2), if a change is requested to a *security* requirement, then the above query expression will retrieve the *read an email message* functionality, all derived main and alternative scenarios, and the events *select a message* and *open the selected message*, as well as the methods *m3* and *m4*.

5.3.3 Impact of Changes to NFRs on Lower-/Higher-Level NFRs

The change to one NFR can migrate down to offspring NFRs or up to parent NFRs in a recursive manner through the decomposition links. This type of traceability enables the analyst to understand the impact of lower-level change on high-level goals, and vice versa. The following Datalog expression implements this query:

TEMP_1 (B,C) ← NFR_DECOMPOSITION (A, B, C, D), B = (NFR_CHANGED)
TEMP_1 (B,C) ← NFR_DECOMPOSITION (A, B, C, D), C = (NFR_CHANGED)
TEMP_1 (B, C) ← NFR_DECOMPOSITION (A, B, C, D), TEMP_1 (X, B)
RESULT (X) = TEMP_1(X, Y), X <> (NFR_CHANGED)
RESULT(Y) = TEMP_1(X,Y), Y <> (NFR_CHANGED)

In the mobile email system (see Figure 5-2), if a change is requested to a *space* requirement, then the above query expression will retrieve the *primary space*, *secondary space*, and *performance* requirements.

5.3.4 Impact of Changes on Interacting Associations

To complete intra-model traceability, it is necessary to establish traces between interacting NFRs at certain association points (interacting associations). The following Datalog expression implements this query:

RESULT(Y) ← NFR_INTERACTION (X,Y,Z,W), Z = "CHANGED_NFR".
RESULT(Z) ← NFR_INTERACTION (X,Y,Z,W) , Y= "CHANGED_NFR".

In the mobile email system (see Figure 5-2), if a change is requested to a *space* requirement at *read email message* functionality, then the above query expression will retrieve the *security* requirement at that functionality.

5.4 Alternative Implementation: XML-Based representation and XQuery implementation

In this section, we provide an alternative implementation for the NFRs tracing queries and we use the XML models to instantiate the proposed metamodel and represent tracing information. We instantiate the metamodel by defining the XML-document structure according to the metamodel in the Document Type Definition (DTD) shown in Figures 5-3 to 5-5.

```
<!ELEMENT NFRs (NFR+)>
<!ATTLIST NFRs
name CDATA #REQUIRED
>
<!ELEMENT NFR (NFRname, interaction?, association?,
operationalization?)>
<!ATTLIST NFR
NFRid ID #REQUIRED
type CDATA #REQUIRED
>
<!ELEMENT NFRname (#PCDATA)>
<!ELEMENT association (functionalelement | FR,
associationcontract)*>
<!ELEMENT functionalelement (#PCDATA)>
<!ELEMENT FR (#PCDATA)>
<!ELEMENT associationcontract (#PCDATA)>
<!ELEMENT interaction (interactingwith)>
<!ATTLIST interaction
associationpint CDATA #REQUIRED
>
<!ELEMENT interactingwith (#PCDATA)>
<!ELEMENT operationalization (op)>
<!ELEMENT op (#PCDATA)>
```

Figure 5- 3: DTD structure representation for NFRs.

```
<!ELEMENT FRs (FR+)>
<!ATTLIST FRs
name CDATA #REQUIRED
>
<!ELEMENT FR (FRname, realization)>
<!ATTLIST FR
```

```
FRid ID #REQUIRED
>
<!ELEMENT FRname (#PCDATA)>
<!ELEMENT realization (realizingelement+)>
<!ELEMENT realizingelement (realizingelement*)>
<!ATTLIST realizingelement
realizingelementid ID #REQUIRED
>
```

Figure 5-4: DTD structure representation for FR.

```
<!ELEMENT NFRDecomposition (RootNFR+)>
<!ATTLIST NFRDecomposition
name CDATA #REQUIRED
>
<!ELEMENT RootNFR (decomposition)>
<!ATTLIST RootNFR
NFRid ID #REQUIRED
>
<!ELEMENT decomposition (subnfr+)>
<!ELEMENT subnfr (subnfr*,)>
<!ATTLIST subnfr
subnfrid ID #REQUIRED
type CDATA #REQUIRED
```

Figure 5-5: DTD structure representation for NFR decomposition.

As an alternative to Datalog queries, we use XQuery [XQUERY] to operate on the data to yield the desired results of tracing information. XQuery is a full-blown functional programming language with strong typing. The evaluation of the query expression reads a sequence of XML fragments or atomic values and returns a sequence of XML fragments or atomic values that are the query result.

The following XQuery expressions implement the tracing query for the impact of changes to functional models on NFRs:

```
//FR_CHANGED refers to ID of the changed functionality.
<result>
{
for $x in doc("NFRs.xml")/NFRs/NFR
where $x/association/FR = "FR_CHANGED"
return data($x/@NFRid)
}
</result>
```

```
<result>
{
for $c in (
for $x in doc("FRs.xml")/FRs/FR
where $x/@FRid = "FR_CHANGED"
return data($x/realization/realizingelement/descendant-orself::
realizingelement/@realizingelementid))
for $b in doc("NFRs.xml")/NFRs/NFR
where $b/association/functionalelement = $c
return data($b/@NFRid)
}
</result>
```

The following XQuery expression implements the tracing query for impact of changes to non-functional models on functional models:

```
<result>
{for $x in doc("NFRs.xml")/NFRs/NFR
where $x/@NFRid ="NFR_CHANGED"
return data($x/association/FR union
$x/association/functionalelement)
}
</result>
```

The following XQuery expression implements the tracing query for the impact of changes to NFRs on lower/ higher-level NFRs:

```
//NFR_CHANGED refers to ID of the changed NFR.
<result>
{
for $x in doc("NFRs.xml")/NFRDecomposition/RootNFR
where $x/@NFRid = "NFR_CHANGED"
or $x/decomposition/subnfr/@subnfrid =
"NFR_CHANGED"
return $x
}
</result>
```

The following XQuery expression implements the tracing query for the impact of changes on interacting associations:

```
<result>
{for $x in doc("NFRs.xml")/NFRs/NFR
where $x/@NFRid ="NFR_CHANGED"
return data( $x/interaction/interactingwith)
}
,
```

```
{
for $x in
doc("NFRs.xml")/NFRs/NFR/interaction/interactingwith
where $x = "NFR_CHANGED"
return data($x)
}
</result>
```

5.5 Traceability Mechanism

NFR tracing occurs through three distinct activities: requirement development, impact detection, and evaluation/decision-making. Each activity ensures that FR and NFRs are treated jointly and in an integrated fashion. These activities are depicted in Figure 5-6.

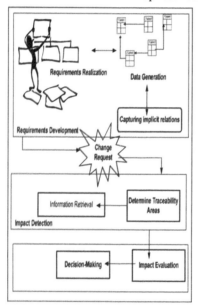

Figure 5-6: NFR-Tracing Activities.

Impact detection is dependent on the effectiveness of the traceability mechanism in establishing correct links between functional and non-functional models and within their corresponding hierarchical models.

Triggered by a change request, the potentially impacted area has to be identified of the requirements along with their specifications and refinements have to be identified, and then the corresponding query should be executed. Once the retrieval algorithm has returned a set of potentially impacted requirements/elements, the evaluation phase can commence. To analysts, this means they can now filter the retrieved requirements/elements to remove any non-relevant ones. A decision on any accepted change in any of the retrieved data should be recorded in the corresponding relations.

It is important to note that one change request can establish a chain of other requests. For example, the need to change one FR may generate the need to accept changes to other NFRs. In response to the NFR changes, the analysts may well see a need to change further sub-NFRs or interacting NFRs.

5.6 Evaluation and Demonstration of the Improvements due to Traceability Queries

For the purpose of the evaluation of the traceability approach, we used the settings from the NOKIA Mobile Email Application System (see Chapter 3, Section 3.3.1) to run a multi project variation experiment. The NOKIA mobile email application is deployed on hundreds of branded cell phones. Change requests are received from the email providers, operators or upon a defect discovery. As a testing practice in NOKIA, upon triggered changes in the requirements, the fix procedure starts and it involves a sanity testing activity. Sanity test is a brief run-through of the functionality of the software system to assure that the system works as expected. The activity is carried on by an execution of a fixed set of sanity test cases (25 test-cases out of more than 10,000 implemented test-cases) to validate that the implemented changes didn't break other features. Of course, the small number of test-cases is due to limitation of time and available human-resources. The objective of the experiment was to evaluate the hypothesis we built to evaluate our approach: "Applying the traceability mechanism proposed in this chapter into the software testing phase will improve the productivity of the testing team; that is for a less test-cases to be executed within a given amount of time, a higher number of defects will be detected". For the purpose of evaluating our traceability approach, we first, linked the requirements and the design solutions into their corresponding test-cases. Second, upon a change request that falls into one of the identified critical areas (see sections 5.3.1 to 5.3.4 of this chapter), the potentially affected requirements, design solutions were retrieved by executing the recommended queries. Third, the corresponding test-cases which are linked to the retrieved requirements and design solutions were selected from the test-cases database. This is of course in addition to the test-cases which are directly linked to the requirement which is referred to by the requested change. The set of selected test-cases was executed in addition and in isolation of the fixed set of sanity test-cases. The results were then compared. This experiment was carried out by the same team of client testers at NOKIA-Montreal office on multiple mobile email projects for a period of nine months from July 2008 till March 2009. The number of the dynamically generated test-cases to be executed varied in each run depending on the triggered change.

To understand the improvements which the use of traceability queries brings to the test-cases selection, we compare the number of test-cases being executed and the number of failed test-cases (each failed test-case prompts the tester to create a defect) between the testing practice using a fixed set of test-cases against using dynamically generated test-cases with the help of our traceability queries. Table 5-1 shows the results which were collected out of 40 test-executions (this is the total number of requests for sanity tests on branded devices at the NOKIA-Montreal office between July 2009 and March 2009). As Table 5-1 indicates, the average number of defects being discovered per sanity-test execution using the dynamically generated test-cases method is 1.825, while it is 0.775 using the fixed set of sanity test-cases. This is an increase of 235%. In addition, the average number of dynamically generated test-cases is less by 33%. These results demonstrate validated the stated hypothesis that the traceability queries were useful in improving the productivity of the testing practice. Figures 5-7 and 5-8 provide visual presentation for the above results.

Table 5-1: Collected Results from Test Executions of NOKIA Mobile Email Application.

ID	Number of test-cases executed (Sanity)	Failed Test-cases	Dynamically generated test-cases	Failed test-cases
1	25	0	11	3
2	25	0	13	2
3	25	0	31	3
4	25	0	21	4
5	25	1	5	0
6	25	0	31	1
7	25	2	31	1
8	25	3	12	3
9	25	2	17	3
10	25	1	12	2
11	25	0	29	3
12	25	2	24	3
13	25	0	23	4
14	25	3	24	5
15	25	0	25	1
16	25	1	18	2
17	25	2	16	2
18	25	4	14	3
19	25	2	5	3
20	25	0	19	2

21	25	0	27	3
22	25	0	13	0
23	25	0	25	0
24	25	0	19	2
25	25	1	19	1
26	25	1	17	2
27	25	1	20	2
28	25	0	35	3
29	25	0	11	1
30	25	0	15	0
31	25	0	16	0
32	25	0	17	0
33	25	1	13	0
34	25	2	14	2
35	25	1	19	1
36	25	1	21	3
37	25	0	23	1
38	25	0	14	0
39	25	0	23	2
40	25	0	28	0
AVERAGE				
	25	0.775	19.25	1.825

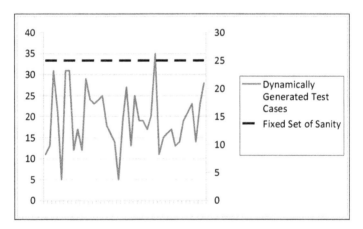

Figure 5-7: Number of Executed Test-Cases: Dynamically Generated Test-Cases vs. Fixed Set of Sanity.

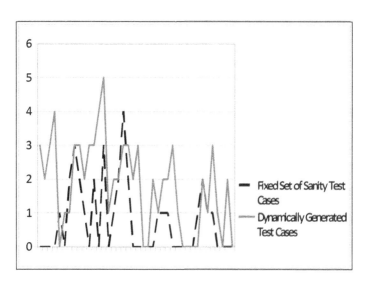

Figure 5-8: Number of Defects: Dynamically Generated Test-Cases vs. Fixed Set of Sanity.

5.7 Conclusion

The tendency for NFRs to have a wide-ranging impact on a software system, and the strong interdependencies and tradeoffs that exist between NFRs and the software architecture, leave typical existing traceability methods incapable of tracing them. In this chapter, we use the NFRs Ontology specification for requirement relations in a real life industrial setting. We proposed and deployed a traceability mechanism under the umbrella of the relational model and the XML models to track the allocation of requirements to system components, and control changes to the system.

One of the advantages of our approach is that it forces system analysts to think about and capture the hierarchical relations within NFRs, the hierarchical relations within FRs, and the relations between NFR and FR hierarchies. Our approach helps systems analysts understand the relationships that exist within and across NFRs in the various phases of development. The chapter proposes a method for tracing a change applied to an NFR in the traceability model, which results in a "slice" of the model containing all model entities immediately reachable from that NFR within the hierarchy. The approach has been evaluated and demonstrated its applicability through a multi project variation experiment performed against the Mobile Email application in NOKIA-Montreal.

Chapter VI: Software Effort Estimation based on Functional and Non-Functional Requirements

"Managing resources is hard; managing them efficiently is even harder."

M. Kircher and P. Jain, 2004

6.1 Introduction

Early in a project, specific details of the nature of the software to be built, details of specific requirements, of the solution, of the staffing needs, and other project variables, are unclear. The variability in these factors contributes to the uncertainty of project effort estimates. As the sources of variability are further investigated and pinned down, the variability in the project diminishes, and so the variability in the project effort estimates can also diminish. This phenomenon is known as the Cone of Uncertainty [Mcc06]. Figure 6-1 shows a sample Cone of Uncertainty based on common project milestones.

In practice, the software development industry, as a whole, has a disappointing track record when it comes to completing a project on time and within budget. The Standish Group published its well-known Chaos Report in 2009 in which it was noted that only 32% of software projects are completed successfully within the estimated schedule and budget [STANDISH09].

Software developers are constantly under pressure to deliver on time and on budget. As a result, many projects focus on delivering functionalities at the expense of meeting NFRs such as reliability, security, maintainability, portability, accuracy, operating constraints among others. As software complexity grows and clients' demands on software quality increase, NFRs can no longer be considered of secondary importance. Many systems fail or fall into disuse precisely because of inadequacies in NFRs [FD96], [BLF99], [LT93] and [MERCEDES97]. While these requirements have always been a concern among software engineering researchers, early work has tended to view NFRs as properties of the finished software product to be evaluated and measured. The lack of effort estimation approaches which take into account the effect of the NFRs on early effort estimation contributes to the Cone of Uncertainty phenomenon. In fact, experiences show that NFRs may represent more than 50% of the total effort to produce services [IBM].

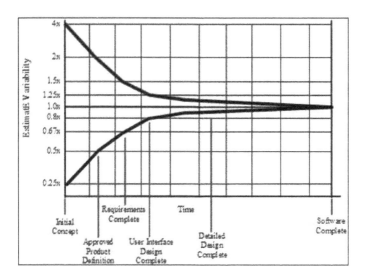

Figure 6-1: The Cone of Uncertainty Based on Common Project Milestones [Mcc06].

The goal of this chapter is to investigate requirements and project-level-tuned early estimation of the software effort with the intent to reduce the effect of the Cone of Uncertainty phenomenon.

As effort is a function of size [PWL05], one way to respond to the need to deal comprehensively and objectively with the effect of NFRs on the scope of a software project is in terms of their corresponding functional size when applicable. Yet, some NFRs cannot have their functional size directly measured. This is mainly because either these NFRs cannot be operationalized in the first place; or their derived operationalizations are in the form of "architectural decisions"; for example.

In this chapter, we draw around the proposed NFRs Ontology (see Chapter 4), and discuss a proposed process for measuring the effort of building a software project while harmonizing the need to develop both FRs and NFRs taking the above limitations into consideration.

The remainder of this chapter is organized as follows: Section 6.2 provides the necessary background on software size estimation, Section 6.3 discusses the relations between the software size and the effort, Section 6.4 provides a proposed approach towards measuring the functional size of NFRs when applicable, Section 6.5 extends Section 6.4 by providing a proposed process towards measuring the effort of a software project, Section 6.6 illustrates the approach through a case study, and Section 6.7 concludes the chapter.

6.2 Software Size Estimation

Software size is a base measure that is used to calculate project effort, duration and cost. One way to respond to the need to deal comprehensively and objectively with the effect of NFRs on the scope of a software project is in terms of their corresponding size.

Software size estimation is the process of predicting the size of a software product. Accurate size estimation is critical to effectively managing the software development process. The project planner must understand the scope of the software to be built and generate an estimate of its size before a project estimate can be made [Pre97].

Software size can be described in terms of length, complexity and functionality. These three aspects of size are described next.

6.2.1 Aspects of Size

Internal product attributes describe a software product in a way that is dependent only on the product itself [FP97]. One of the most useful attributes is the size of a software product, which can be measured statically without executing the system [FP97]. In the context of project planning, size refers to quantifiable outcome of the software project [Pre97].

Since other physical objects are easily measurable, it might be assumed that measuring the size of software products should be straightforward. In practice, however, size measurement can be difficult [FP97]. Simple measures of size are often rejected because they do not provide adequate information. Those who reject a measure because it does not provide enough information may be expecting too much of a simple measure [FP97].

For example, if a human size is measured as a single attribute such as weight, then we can determine the number of people who can safely ride in an elevator at one time. However we cannot determine whether passengers will bump their head on the elevator door. If human size is measured in terms of two attributes such as weight and height, then we can determine both the number of people who can safely ride in an elevator at one time and whether passengers will bump their head on the elevator door.

Similarly, if software size is measured in terms of the number of LOC, the fact that it is not useful in measuring quality does not negate its value [FP97]. Rather this might indicate a requirement for more information.

It is therefore often useful to define an external attribute such as size in terms of more than one internal attribute. Applying measures to different goals does not invalidate them for their original purpose [FP97]. Ideally, we want to define a set of views for software size. Each view should capture a key aspect of software size. Fenton suggests that software size can be described with three views: length, complexity, and functionality [FP97]. A summary on these three views is provided below.

6.2.1.1 Length

Length is the physical size of the product. There are three major development products whose size would be useful to know: the specification, the design and the code. The length of the specification can indicate how long the design is likely to be, which in turn is a predictor of code length [FP97].

6.2.1.1.1 Length of Code

The most commonly used measure of source code program length is the number of LOC [FP97]. Many different approaches to counting LOC have been proposed. The software engineering Institute has developed a set of guidelines to help in deciding how to measure LOC [Par92]. This recommendation is flexible in that it allows you to tailor the definition of LOC for your needs [FP97].

6.2.1.1.2 Length of Specifications and Design

Specification and design documents may use text, graphs, or mathematical diagrams and symbols to express information. In measuring code length, an atomic object must be identified to count (LOC, executable statements, source instructions, operators and operands). Similarly, for specification and design documents, one or more objects are identified and counted [FP97].
In the case of dataflow diagrams, objects such as processes (bubble nodes), external entities (box nodes), data stores (line nodes), and data flows (arcs) are counted [Pre97]. In case of class diagram, objects such as classes are counted. It is common in industry to use the number of pages to measure length for documents containing text and graphs [FP97].

6.2.1.2 Complexity

Complexity can be interpreted in different ways. In the context of software size, complexity refers to algorithmic complexity and problem complexity [FP97].

6.2.1.2.1 Problem Complexity

Problem complexity (also called Computational complexity) is branch of the theory of computation in computer science that focuses on classifying problems according to their inherent difficulty. Here, a problem is understood in the narrow sense of a task that is in principle amenable to be solved by a computer. Informally, a problem is regarded as inherently difficult if solving the problem requires a large amount of resources, independent of the algorithm used for solving it. The theory formalizes this intuition, by introducing mathematical models of computation and casting computational tasks mathematically as decision problems. The degree of difficulty can be quantified in the amount of resources needed to solve these problems, such as time and storage. In particular, the theory seizes the practical limits on what computers can and cannot do.

6.2.1.2.2 Algorithmic Complexity

Algorithmic complexity reflects the complexity of the algorithm used to solve the problem [FP97]. A key distinction between computational complexity theory and analysis of algorithm is that the latter is devoted on analyzing the amount of resources needed by a particular algorithm to solve a concrete problem, whereas the former asks a more general question. Namely, it targets at classifying problems that can, or cannot, be solved with appropriately restricted resources. A mathematical notation called **big-O notation** is used to define an order relation on functions. The big-O form of a function is derived by finding the dominating term $f(n)$. Big-O notation captures the asymptotic behavior of the function. Using this notation, the efficiency of algorithm A is $O(f(n))$, where, for input size n, algorithm A required at most $O(f(n))$ operations in the worst case [FP97].

For example, the function

$$f(n) = 3n^2 + 2n + 26$$

is big-O n^2 written as $O(n^2)$. The algorithm will therefore requires at most $O(n^2)$ operations.

The methods to measure the length and complexity aspects of the size have the following limitations [ISO1414398]:

1. These methods cannot always be applied in the early phases of software development life cycles.

2. These methods cannot always be understood by the user of the software.

To overcome above mentioned limitations, methods that are not based on length or complexity have been proposed. Most of the methods that are used today to measure the size of the software are based upon the "Functionality" of the software [GD08]. These methods measure the size of the software by measuring the functionality that it provides to the customer.

6.2.1.3 Functionality

Functional Size Methods (FSMs) have shifted the focus from measuring the technical characteristics of the software towards measuring the functionality of the software that is required by the intended users of the software. It is important to note that functional size is the only standardized way to measure the software size [Foro4]. This method is independent of the development tools and the programming languages. It is also independent of the technical requirements of the software.

For the above reasons, we will be referring in this chapter to the "functionality" aspect of size when we deal with the size of a requirement or a project.

The first method; named Function Points, which calculates the functionality of the software is designed in 1979 by Albrecht [Alb79]. Function Point Analysis method (FPA) [GD08] served as bases for the first FSM industrial method. Over the years, different variations and varieties of FSM methods have emerged. A preview evolution of FSM methods is presented in Table 6-1:

Table 6-1: Concepts, FSM Methods and Description (adapted from [ISO1414398] and [GD08]).

Year	Method Name	Developer
1979	Albrecht FPA/IFPUG FPA	[AG83] and [Alb84] / International Function Point Users Group (IFPUG) [IFPUG99] and [ISO2092603]
1982	DeMarco's Bang Metrics	DeMarco [Dem82]
1986	Feature Points	Jones [Jon87]
1988	MK II FPA	Symons [Sym88], The United Kingdom Software Metrics Association (UKSMA) [ISO2096802] and [MKII98]
1990	NESMA FPA	The Netherlands Software Metrics Users Association (NESMA) [NESMA97] and [ISO2457005].
1990	Asset-R	Reifer [Rei90].
1992	3-D FP	Whitmire [Whi92].
1994	Object Points	Banker et al [BKWZ94].Kauffmn and Kumar [KK97].
1994	FP by Matson, Barret and Mellichamp	Matson et al. [MBM94]
1997	Full Function Points (FFP)	University of Quebec in cooperation with the Software Engineering Lab. in Applied Metrics [ASMD98].
1997	Early FPA (EFPA)	Meli [Mel97a] and [Mel97b], Conte et al. [CIMS04]
1998	Object Oriented FP	Caldiera et al. [CAFL98]
1999	Predictive OP	Teologlou [Teo99]
1999	COSMIC FFP	The Common Software Measurement Consortium

		(COSMIC) [Abr99] and [ISO1976103].
2000	Early and Quick COSMIC FFP	Meli et al [MAHO00], Conte et al. [CIMS04]
2000	Kammelar's Component OP	Kammelar [Kam00]
2001	Object Oriented Method FP	Pastor et al. [PAMT01]
2004	FiSMA FSM	The Finnish Software Metrics Association (FiSMA) [For04]

For the purposes of this research, we have chosen to use the COSMIC FSM method [ADOSS03] developed by the Common Software Measurement International Consortium (COSMIC) and now adopted as an international standard [ISO1976103]. We chose this method in particular because it conforms to all ISO requirements [ISO1414389] for functional size measurement, and addresses some of the major theoretical weaknesses of the earlier FPA techniques like Albrecht's FPs [AG83]. The COSMIC method is described in the next section.

6.2.2 The COSMIC Method

The FSM method developed by the Common Software Measurement International Consortium (COSMIC) has now been adopted as an international standard (ISO 19761 [ISO1976103]) and is referred to as the COSMIC method [ADOSS03]. This measurement method has been designed to measure the functional size of management information systems, real-time software and multi-layer systems. Its design conforms to all ISO requirements (ISO 14143-1 [ISO1414398]) for FSM methods, and was developed to address some of the major weaknesses of earlier methods, like FPA [AR94], the design of which dates back almost 30 years, to a time when software was much smaller and much less varied. COSMIC focuses on the "user view" of functional requirements and is applicable throughout the development life cycle, right from the requirements phase to the implementation and maintenance phases. Before starting to measure using the COSMIC method, it is imperative to carefully define the purpose, the scope and the measurement viewpoint. This may be considered as the first step of the measurement process. The measurer defines why the measurement is being undertaken, and/or what the result will be, as well as the set of functionalities to be included in a specific FSM exercise. Measurements taken using the COSMIC method with a different purpose and scope and a different measurement viewpoint may therefore give quite a different size.

In the measurement of software functional size using the COSMIC method, the software functional processes and their triggering events must be identified [ISO1976103] and

[ADOSS03]. In COSMIC, the unit of measurement is a data movement, which is a base functional component that moves one or more data attributes belonging to a single data group. Data movements can be of four types: Entry, Exit, Read or Write. The functional process is an elementary component of a set of user requirements triggered by one or more triggering events either directly or indirectly via an actor. It comprises at least two data movement types: an Entry plus at least either an Exit or a Write The triggering event is an event occurring outside the boundary of the measured software and initiates one or more functional processes. The subprocesses of each functional process are sequences of events. An Entry moves a data group, which is a set of data attributes, from a user across the boundary into the functional process, while an Exit moves a data group from a functional process across the boundary to the user requiring it. A Write moves a data group lying inside the functional process to persistent storage, and a Read moves a data group from persistent storage to the functional process. See Figure 6-2 for an illustration of the generic flow of data attributes through software from a functional perspective.

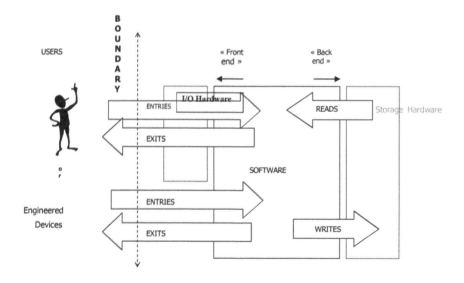

Figure 6-2: Generic Flow of Data Attributes through Software from a Functional Perspective [ADOSS03].

A general procedure for measuring software functional size with the COSMIC method is proposed in [AOA04], as in Figure 6-3. The measurement process is performed in five steps.

First, the boundary of the software to be measured is identified by the measurer based on the requirements and the specifications of the interaction between the hardware and the software. Second, the measurer identifies all possible functional processes, triggering events and data groups from the requirements. These are considered as candidate items at this stage. Third, the candidate items (i.e. functional processes, triggering events and data groups) are mapped into the COSMIC software context model (Figure 6-3) based on the COSMIC rules. In this mapping, each functional process must be associated with a triggering event and to the data group(s) manipulated by it. This mapping also allows the identification of layers. Fourth, the COSMIC subprocesses (i.e. data movements of the following types: Entry, Exit, Read and Write) are identified within each functional process. The COSMIC measurement function is applied to the subprocesses identified to determine their respective COSMIC size measure. Finally, the measurer computes an aggregate of the measurement results to obtain the total functional size of the software being measured.

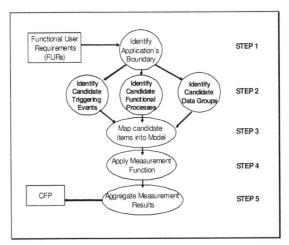

Figure 6-3: General Procedure for Measuring Software Size with the COSMIC Method – ISO 19761 [AOA04].

6.3 The Relationship between Functional Size and Effort

Software cost and effort estimation plays a significant role in the successful completion of any software. Resources are assigned according to the effort required to complete the software. Accurate effort estimation leads the completion of software project on the scheduled time. Many models and approaches have been developed in the past 40 years to estimate the effort. Most of the models take software size as a basic input to estimate the effort [GD08]. We have already discussed that it is better to use functional size instead of length of code to estimate effort. Effort is usually calculated by using functional size of the software [FP97]. There is a strong relationship between functional size and effort [PWL05]. Valid measured functional size has the potential to improve effort estimation and reduce the "cone of uncertainty" effect on the project planning. It is critical to correctly establish a relationship between functional size and effort so that we could be able to estimate effort accurately. There are many project and product factors that affect positively or negatively this relationship. Environmental factors, technical factors and operating constraints are some of them [Gen08].

Many significant attempts have been taken to explore the relationship between the size and effort and also to identify the subset of those NFRs which may affect this relation. In the sections 6.3.1 to 6.3.8, we present an overview of research studies, effort estimation models and functional size estimation methods which consider NFRs as factors affecting the relationship between the software size and effort:

6.3.1 Study by Maxwell and Forselius

A study carried out in Finnish companies [MF00] to explore the factors that affect productivity and effort estimation shows the following results (Table 6-2):

Table 6-2: Factors Affecting Productivity by Pekka Forselius (adapted from [MF00]).

Data set	Experience Database (206 business software projects from 26 companies).
Variables considered in Database Productivity Analysis	Application Programming Language, Application Type (MIS etc), Hardware Platform, User Interface, Development Model, DBMS Architecture, DB Centralization, Software Centralization, DBMS Tools, Case Cools, Operating System, Company where project was developed, Business Sector (Banking, Insurance etc), Customer Participation, Staff Availability,

	Standard Use, Method Use, Tool Use, Software Logical Complexity, Requirement Volatility, Quality Requirement, Efficiency Requirement, Installation Requirement, Staff's Analysis Skills, Staff's Tools Skills, Staff's Team Skills, Staff's Application Knowledge
Base of Size Measurement	Experience 2.0 Function Point Method

6.3.2 Study by Angelis, Stamelos and Morisio

L. Angelis and his colleagues have also made important contribution towards finding the different factors that affect size and effort relationship. These authors study the projects in the International Software Benchmarking Standards Group (ISBSG). The ISBSG database contains data about recently developed projects characterized mostly by attributes of categorical nature such as the project business area, organization type, application domain and usage of certain tools or methods. The authors found 7 important factors that affect the relationship between the size and effort. The result of this study is given in more detail below (Table 6-3) [ASM01]:

Table 6-3: Factors Affecting Productivity by L. Angelis [ASM01].

Data set	ISBSG release 6
Factors	1. Development Type 2. Development Platform 3. Language Type 4. Used Methodology 5. Organization Type 6. Business Area Type 7. Application Type
Base of Size Measurement	IFPUG Function Point

The authors' method is based on the characterization of the software to be developed in terms of project and environment attributes and comparison with some similar completed projects recovered from the ISBSG.

The authors also refer to that human factors are very important factors that are not taken into account while performing any previous study. A recent study shows that Psychometrics data should be collected to better perform the empirical study [FTAS08].

6.3.3 Study by Liebchen and Shepperd

A study by Liebchen and Shepperd that aims at reporting on an ongoing investigation into software productivity and its influencing factors brought the following results (Table 6-4) [LS05]:

Table 6-4: Factors Affecting Productivity by Martin Shepperd [LS05].

Data Set	25,000 closed projects of a large multinational company
Attributes Influencing Software Productivity	1. The Degree of Technical Innovation, Business Innovation, Application Innovation, 2. Team Complexity 3. Client Complexity 4. Degree of Concurrency 5. Development Team Degree of Experience With Tools, Information Technology, Hardware, or With Adopted Methodology, 6. The Project Management Experience
Base of Size Measurement	Function Point

This study confirms the intuitive notion that different industry sectors exhibit the differences in the productivity. It is due to the fact that industry sectors also affect the productivity [LS05].

6.3.4 Summary of Other Studies

A study in the different Swedish companies shows that following factors affect the effort estimation [MP08]:

1. Requirement Volatility (Unclear and Changing Requirement).

2. Unavailability of Templates.

3. Lack of coordination between product developed and other parts of the project.

The following factors that are considered important from ISBSG data repository, also affect the productivity [LWHS01]:

1. Programming Language.

2. Team Size.

3. Organization Type.

4. Application Type.

Another recent study published in the Second ACM-IEEE international Symposium on Empirical Software Engineering and Measurement shows the following results (Table 6-5) [YHLWB08]:

Table 6-5: Factors Affecting Phase Distribution for Software Development Effort [YHLWB08].

Data Set	China Software Benchmarking Standard Group
Factors	1. Development Life Cycle 2. Development Size 3. Software Size 4. Team Size
Base for Size Measurement	LOC

By analyzing the factors collected from the above studies, we find that all of them are mapped to concepts under the root of the *NonFunctionalRequirement* concept in our NFRs Ontology (Chapter 4). In sections 6.4, 6.5 and 6.6 of this chapter, we discuss how to quantify the impact of these factors on the size – effort relationship.

6.3.5 Factors in the Use Case Points estimation method (UCP)

UCP method is based on a work by Gustav Karner [Kar93]. This method analyzes the use case actors, scenarios, and various technical and environmental factors and abstract them into an equation. Readers familiar with Allan Albrecht's FPA [Alb79], [AG83] and [Alb84] will recognize its influence on UCP; function point analysis inspired UCP. The UCP equation is composed of three variables:

    a. Unadjusted Use Case Points (UUCP).

    b. The Technical Complexity Factor (TCF). (Table 6-6)

    c. The Environmental Complexity Factor (ECF). (Table 6-7)

Table 6-6: Technical Complexity Factors in UCP.

1. Distributed System	8. Portability
2. Performance	9. Easy to change
3. End User Efficiency	10. Concurrency
4. Complex Internal Processing	11. Special security features
5. Reusability	12. Provides direct access to third parties
6. Easy to Install	13. Special user training facilities are required
7. Easy to Use	

Table 6-7: Environmental Complexity Factors in UCP.

1. Familiar with UML	5. Object-Oriented Experience
2. Part-Time Workers	6. Motivation
3. Analyst Capability	7. Difficult Programming Language
4. Application Experience	8. Stable Requirements

According to the UCP method, TCF can reduce the UCP by 40 percent and increase the UCP by 30 percent. On the other hand, the ECF can reduce the UCP by 57.5 percent and increase the UCP y 40 percent.

A study by [ABH05] which was based on the UCP method, suggests that this method needs modification to better handle effort related to the development process and the quality of the code.

6.3.6 Cost Drivers in COCOMO 81

COCOMO [Boe81]; developed by Barry Boehm, is a model for estimating effort and calendar time required to develop a software system. At the most basic level COCOMO is two equations:

$$Effort = f(x,y) \text{ and}$$

$$Time = g(effort),$$

where f() and g() are functions and x and y are attributes of the system. Original COCOMO is a three level model: (i) Basic, (ii) Intermediate and (iii) Detailed which calculates the effort per phase.

The development period covered by COCOMO begins after requirements and continues through integration and testing.

Intermediate COCOMO computes software development effort as function of program size and a set of "cost drivers" that include subjective assessment of product, hardware, personnel and project attributes. Table 6-8 presents the 15 cost drivers that have linear effect on estimated effort:

Table 6-8: Cost Drivers in COCOMO 81.

1. Required Software Reliability	9. Applications Experience
2. Data Base Size	10. Programmer Capability
3. Software Complexity	11. Virtual Machine experience
4. Execution Time Constraint	12. Programming Language Experience
5. Main Storage Constraint	13. Use of Modern Programming Practices
6. Virtual Machine Volatility	14. Use of Software Tools
7. Computer Turnaround Time	15. Schedule Constraints
8. Analyst Capability	

Each of the 15 attributes receives a rating on a six-point scale that ranges from "very low" to "extra high" (in importance or value). There are tables of values used to determine effort multipliers for each of these cost drivers in each rating. For example, the programmer capability multiplier ranges from 1.42 (low skill) to 0.7 (high skill). These values will raise or lower the overall figures. The results of the effort formulas above are multiplied by the effort multipliers to arrive at the final result. The product of all effort multipliers results in an *effort adjustment factor (EAF)*. Typical values for EAF range from 0.9 to 1.4.

6.3.7 Cost drivers in COCOMO II

The original COCOMO model has been very successful, but it doesn't apply to newer software development practices as well as it does to traditional practices. COCOMO II [BAB+00] was updated for current development models (iterative and incremental; i.e. non waterfall). COCOMO II incorporates an early estimation equations based on function points [IFPUG99] and [ISO209260J] or object points. COCOMO II is adjustable for non-linear effects and includes updates to effort-multipliers and cost drivers. In addition, requirements volatility is considered. In COCOMO II, phases or levels are in:

(i)   Early prototyping Level: Pre-requirements

(ii)   Early Design Level – Requirements and some design complete:

This model is to be used for rough estimates of a project's cost and duration before entire architecture is determined. It uses a small set of new Cost Drivers, and new estimating equations. It is based on Unadjusted Function Points or KSLOC (1,000 Source Lines Of Code). COCOMO II defines 7 early design cost drivers shown in Table 6-9:

Table 6-9: Cost Drivers in COCOMO II Early Design Model.

1. Product Reliability and Complexity	5. Personnel Experience
2. Developed for Reusability	6. Facilities
3. Platform Difficulty	7. Required Development Schedule
4. Personnel Capability and Mapping Example	

(iii)   Post Architecture Level – System design and architecture established

This is the most detailed COCOMO II model. It is to be used after project's overall architecture is developed. It has new cost drivers, new line counting rules, and new equations. COCOMO II defines 17 post-architecture cost drivers shown in Table 6-10:

Table 6-10: Cost Drivers in COCOMO II Post Architecture Model.

1. Product Reliability	10. Programmer Capability
2. Database Size	11. Personnel Continuity
3. Product Complexity	12. Applications Experience
4. Developed for Reusability	13. Platform Experience
5. Documentation Match to Life-Cycle Needs	14. Language and tool Experience
6. Execution Time Constraints	15. Use of Software Tools
7. Main Storage Constraint	16. Multi-set Development
8. Platform Volatility	17. Required Development Schedule
9. Analyst Capability	

6.3.8 Discussion

Existing FSM methods have been primarily focused on sizing the functionality of a software system. Size measures are expressed as single numbers (function points (FP) [ISO2092603], [ISO2457005], [ASMD98] and [UKSMA02]), or multidimensional 'arrays' designed to reflect how many of certain types of items there are in a system [Ste01]. The existing function-point-based FSM techniques have so far addressed the topic of NFRs only with respect to the task of adjusting the (unadjusted) FP counts to the project context or the environment in which the system is supposed to work.

For example, the International Function Point Users Group (IFPUG) [IFPUG] has been approaching the inclusion of NFRs in the final FP count by using qualitative judgments about the system's environment. The current version of the IFPUG Function Point Analysis (FPA) manual [IFPUG99] speaks of a set of General System Characteristics and Value Adjustment Factors (see Table 6-11) all meant to address – though in different ways – the NFRs that a project may include.

Table 6-11: General System Characteristics in IFPUG.

1. Reliable back-up and recovery	8. Online Update
2. Data communications	9. Complex Interface
3. Distributed functions	10. Complex Processing
4. Performance	11. Reusability
5. Heavily used configuration	12. Installation ease
6. Online data entry	13. Multiple Sites
7. Operational ease	14. Facilitate Change

Currently, there are five FSM models which are proposed by the COSMIC consortium and IFPUG member associations (namely, NESMA [ISO2457005], UKSMA [UKSMA02], COSMIC [Abr99], FISMA [FISMA08] and IFPUG [IFPUG99]) and which are recognized as ISO standards. We compared and contrasted the ways in which NFRs are treated in these FSM standards. For each standard, we looked at what NFR artifact is used as input to the FSM process, how this artifact is evaluated (Table 6-12), and which FSM counting component reflects the NFRs. We found that all five FSM standards provide, at best, checklists which estimators can use to perform qualitative assessments of certain factors of the system's environment. However, these assessments reflect the subjective view of the professionals who run the FSM process. The FSM standards say nothing about what should be put in place to enable estimators to ensure the reproducibility of their assessment results regarding the NFRs in a project. The Mark II FPA manual [UKSMA02] refers to recent statistical analysis results and suggests that neither the Value Adjustment Factors from the IFPUG method [ISO2092603] nor the Technical Complexity Adjustment (TCA) factors from the Mark II FPA method [UKSMA02] represent well the influence on size of the various characteristics these two methods try to take into account. Indeed, the Mark II FPA manual says that the TCA factors are included only because of continuity with previous versions, and recommends that these factors be ignored altogether (p. 63 in [ISO1414398]) when sizing applications within a single technical environment (where the TCA is likely to be constant).

Table 6-12: The ISO FSM Standards.

Proposal	Input NFR artifact	Assessment	Counting Component
COSMIC [Abr99]	Not included	Not applicable	None
NESMA [ISO2457005]	Textual NFR	Qualitative	General System Characteristics, Value Adjustment Factors
MARK II [UKSMA02]	Textual NFR	Qualitative	Technical Complexity Adjustment
FISMA [FISMA08]	Textual NFR	Qualitative	Technical Complexity Adjustment
IFPUG [ISO2092603]	Textual NFR	Qualitative	General System Characteristics, Value Adjustment Factors

6.4 Non-Functional Requirements Size Measurement Method (NFSM) with COSMIC

While the COSMIC method was originally proposed to measure user FRs, in this section, we extend its use to measuring the functional size of the operationalized NFRs. Figure 6-4 instantiates the NFRs Ontology in the context of the COSMIC method. In the instantiated metamodel, the major functionalities, as well as the functional operationalizations, are mapped to the COSMIC processes.

The process of measuring the functional size for a particular NFR is carried out in three steps:

Step 1: The NFR is considered in isolation from its association relations. COSMIC is used to measure the functional size for those operationalizations, which are refined from the NFR and correspond to functions/operations. The size of the NFR is the sum of the sizes of all the selected operationalizations.

Step 2: The NFR's association relations with the FRs are clearly captured.

Step 3: The total size of the NFR within the system is then calculated by measuring the total changes in the functional size of functionalities triggered by introducing the associated NFR.

We completed our first application of this procedure in a case study setting at a company site (see Chapter 3, Section 3.3.1). To illustrate the measurement procedure, we will limit the discussion to the same two pieces of functionality: (1) the user asks to read an email message; and (2) the user composes and sends a new email. The specification of these functionalities is illustrated in Figure 6-5. The COSMIC models are generated for each component (here, Client and Gateway), as outlined next:

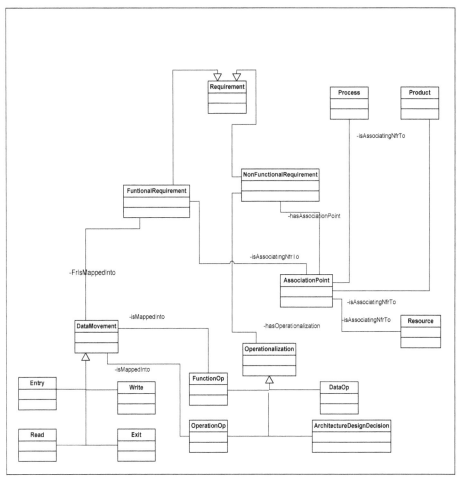

Figure 6-4: A View of the NFRs Ontology Instantiated in the Context of the COSMIC Method.

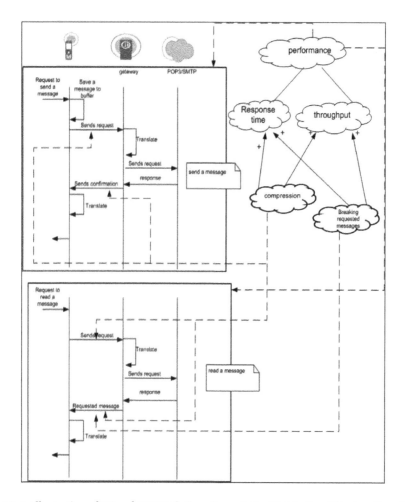

Figure 6-5: Illustration of FR and NFR Relations through the Mobile Email System Case Study.

The chosen FRs, *read email* and *send email*, each consists of two functional processes, which are further refined into data movements (see Figure 6-5). The data groups identified for these read and send FRs are: 1) read request data group (includes data on the requested message); 2) read response data group (includes the message requested to be read); 3) send request data group (includes the composed message to be sent); and 4) send response data group (confirmative message).

The functional size for each FR corresponds to the addition of all identified data movements. The initial calculated functional size for the Client component is 11 CFP (see Tables 6-13 and 6-15) and 12 CFP for the Gateway component (see Tables 6-14 and 6-15).

Table 6-13: Client Component ("Send a Message" Functionality).

ID	Process description	Triggering event	Data Movement	Data Group	Data movement Type	CFP
FP1	Send	Request event	Receive send request	Send request	E	1
			Save message in the buffer	Send request	W	1
			Send message to gateway	Send request	X	1
		Response event	Receive confirmation	Send response	E	1
			Translate message	Send response	W	1
			Display confirmation	Send response	X	1
	Total functional size of Send FUR for Client component in CFP =					6

Table 6-14: Gateway Component ("Send a Message" Functionality).

ID	Process description	Triggering event	Data Movement	Data Group	Data movement Type	CFP
FP 1	Send	Request event	Receive send request	Send request	E	1
			Translate message to IMAP/POP3	Send request	W	1
			Send message to mail server	Send request	X	1
		Response event	Receive confirmation	Send response	E	1
			Translate message to SYNCML	Send response	W	1
			Send confirmation to client	Send response	X	1
Total functional size of Send for Gateway component in CFP =						**6**

Table 6-15: Client Component ("Read a Message" Functionality).

ID	Process description	Triggering event	Data Movement	Data Group	Data movement Type	CFP
FP 2	Read	Request event	Receive read request	Read Request	E	1
			Send message to gateway	Read Request	X	1
		Response event	Receive user's message	Read Response	E	1
			Translate message	Read Response	W	1
			Display message	Read Response	X	1
Total functional size of Read for Client component in CFP =						**5**

Table 6-16: Gateway Component ("Read a Message" Functionality).

ID	Process description	Triggering event	Data Movement	Data Group	Data movement Type	CFP
FP2	Read	Request event	Receive read request	Read Request	E	1
			Translate request to IMAP/POP3	Read Request	W	1
			Send request to mail server	Read Request	X	1
		Response event	Receive user's message	Read Response	E	1
			Translate message to SYNCML	Read Response	W	1
			Send requested message to client	Read Response	X	1
Total functional size of Read for Gateway component in CFP =						**6**

In our case study setting, we observed that, in order to optimize the user experience for devices with limitations (e.g. screen size, memory, processing speed) and wireless networks with constrained bandwidth, some NFRs had to be adapted in the requirements model of the project. To illustrate this point here, we consider adaptation of the performance requirement. Performance is defined as the amount of useful work accomplished by software compared to the time and resources used. To deal effectively with such a requirement, a *good performance* requirement may need to be broken down into smaller components, so that an effective solution can be found. Thus, *performance* can be *decomposed* into *short response time* for the exchanged transactions between the client and the gateway, and *high throughput* (rate of processing work) for the network bandwidth.

After an extensive round of meetings and discussions, the software architects at NOKIA decided to optimize *response time* and *throughput* of the Mobile Email Application by means of the following two solutions: (1) a compression algorithm, which compresses the requests and responses exchanged between the device application and the gateway; and (2) breaking a message requested to be read into smaller pages, each 1 Kb in size, after which only the first page is sent to the client, with the option for the user to request the other pages from the gateway in separate transactions.

The suggested operationalizations proved to reduce the response time as perceived by the end-user in similar projects. They also reduced the amount of wireless traffic. The performance requirement, along with its decomposition, operationalization, and association relations, are depicted in Figure 6-5. The SYNCML protocol compression algorithm reduces the size of the protocol elements or XML markup, and not of the actual email data. The algorithm is based on a static compression dictionary containing a list of the most common protocol fragments. During compression, the source XML message is split up into dictionary and non-dictionary words (logic). A special dictionary is searched (Read) and each fragment that maps to a dictionary word is replaced with the corresponding index (Write). A fragment which does not map to a dictionary word is replaced with its length in bytes using UTF-8 encoding plus 1000 followed by the fragment itself (Write). During decompression, these subprocesses are reversed. In total, the functional size for the compression operationalization is obtained by summing up all the data movements identified. The initial calculated functional size is 3 * 2 = 6 CFP.

The breaking down of a message by the gateway into smaller pages was mapped into three subprocesses: The gateway recognizes that the message size exceeds 1 Kb and decides to break it down into smaller pieces (Entry), the gateway writes the first page of the message into a special buffer to be sent to the client (Write) right away, and then the gateway stores the rest of the message into a special memory (Write) for future requested transactions. The functional size for breaking the message down into pages is 3 CFP.

To calculate the functional size of the performance NFR, we consider the association of the performance requirement and the association of their derived operationalizations, as presented in Figure 6-5. The compression algorithm (including both the compression and the decompression) has to be called once for each data group. This increases the total functional size for both functionalities by (4 * 6 = 24 CFP). In the case of breaking down the message, it is called on once for *read message*. Thus, the functional size of *read message* is increased by 3 CFP. The calculated functional size for performance is, therefore, the sum of the two functional sizes: 24 + 3 = 27 CFP. The updated total functional size for both functionalities (*send a message* and *read a message*) after introducing the performance requirement is 27 + 11 + 12 = 50 CFP.

6.5 Measuring the effort of NFRs

Measuring the functional size of NFRs as presented in our approach falls under the "Count, Compute, Judge" estimation technique [Mcc06], which means, basically, that the first course of action consists of counting and computing. If there is a way to directly count and compute some value to provide the estimate, this should be the best option, since it usually provides the most accurate result. If "count and compute" is not possible, then "judge" is considered, but as a last resort only, as it introduces the greatest opportunity for bias and error.

As illustrated in Section 6.4 of this chapter, The "NFSM" approach is applicable to the NFRs associated with FRs and operationalized through functions/processes which could be mapped to the COSMIC model. Nevertheless, the goal-oriented RE community [Myl06], [Gli05] and [Wie00] considers that not all NFRs should be decomposed into functions/processes. If NFRs serve as norms [Gli05] or as criteria for making architectural design choices, then they should not be decomposed into FRs. Examples are global NFRs like survivability, reporting, and customizability. In this section, we discuss an approach towards measuring the effort estimation of the project while dealing comprehensively with the impact of a particular NFR on the size and effort of the FRs and consequently the size and the effort of software project taking the above limitation into consideration. The proposed approach will benefit from the NFSM method discussed in section 6.4. Specifically, we address this need by: (1) measuring the functional size of the operationalizations in isolation from their relations; (2) understanding and specifying those relations of the NFRs with other system elements; (3) adjusting the functional size of the captured functionalities and the total project using the measurement from (1) and the specification of NFR's relations from (2); and finally (4) when the size of the operationalizations cannot be measured OR the NFRs cannot be refined into design solutions (unoperationalized NFRs), we then consider the impact of these operationalizations and "unoperationalized NFRs" on the size of functionalities and the effort of building the project through an estimation models based on regression techniques.

NFRs and Operationalizations can be further categorized into 4 non-mutually exclusive classes from the perspective of measuring the effort:

(i)   *Class A:* operationalizations which correspond to functions/operations and associated to functional requirements subprocesses;

(ii)   *Class B:* (Atomic NFRs which are not operationalized OR operationalizations corresponding to architectural/design decisions or data) AND associated to functional requirements subprocesses;

(iii)   *Class C:* operationalizations correspond to functions/operations and associated to the whole product, process or resource;

(iv)   *Class D:* (Atomic NFRs which are not operationalized OR operationalizations corresponding to architectural/design decisions or data) AND associated to a whole product, a process or a resource.

Before we proceed in discussing the steps of the process in Section 6.5.2; we will provide a background on the estimation models using regression techniques in Section 6.5.1.

6.5.1 Estimation Models: Background

A model typically describes the relationship between a dependent variable (such as effort) with respect to one or more independent variables (such as size, experience, project difficulty).

When a relationship has been well studied empirically, then the model of such a relationship can be described mathematically with simple (or very complex) mathematical formula. This is the case with many physical phenomena that have been well studied (e.g. gravity, fluidity of liquids, expansion of gases).

One of the most common-in-use estimation techniques [Mcco6] is to build estimations models based on characteristics of the productivity of past projects. If the historical data from past projects is quantitative and documented, then estimation models can be built.

A simple effort estimation model (Effort vs. Size) is illustrated in Figure 6-6 and typically represents the performance of past projects.

- The x axis represents the functional size of the software projects completed;
- The y axis represents the number of effort hours that it took to deliver a software project.

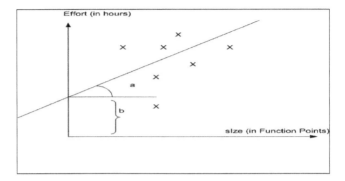

Figure 6-6: Production Model with Fixed Cost and Variable Costs.

The points in the graph in Figure 6-6 represent the number of person-hours it took to deliver the corresponding functional size of the projects completed. The line in the graph is obtained through a linear regression model which basically builds the line that best represents this set of points in terms of effort with respect to the corresponding size.

An effort estimation model is typically built with data from projects completed in the past that is, when:

- All the required information on a project is available.
- There is no more uncertainty in both project inputs and the outputs: all of the software features have been delivered, and
- All of the work hours for the project have been accurately entered in a time reporting system.

In a production process, there are typically two major types of costs:

- Variable costs: The portion of the resources expanded (i.e. inputs) that depends directly on the number of outputs produced. In Figure 6-6, this corresponds to the slope of the model, that is: slope = a (in terms of hours per function point)
- Fixed costs: The portion of resources expanded (e.g. inputs) that do not depend on the number of outputs. In Figure 6-6, this corresponds to b, the constant hours at the origin when the size is equal to zero. There are a number of project management plans, procedures and controls to set-up, as well as standards to be selected and used, independently of the size of the project. In a typical production process, these would be fixed costs of a production run.

A linear model of the relationship between effort and size is represented by the following formula:

Effort in person-hours = a * Size + b

where

Size = number of Function Points (FP)

a = variable Cost and is the number of person-hours per Function Point (person-hours/FP)

b = fixed cost in person-hours.

Figure 6-7 illustrates a production process where there is not a fixed cost: in this situation, the production line goes straight through the origin where effort y = 0 when size x = 0.

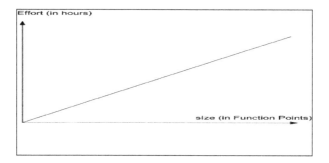

Figure 6-7: Production Model with no Fixed Cost.

To build the estimation models, the linear regression technique is often selected over more complex estimation techniques such as analogy-based and neural network techniques [Abr09] which have not yet been shown to better explain the size-effort relationship in software projects on the types of data sets available for such studies, including multi-organizational data sets.

A survey of the literature [Abr09] on estimation models based on real projects suggests that there is rarely a significant deviation from the linear model in the software effort function. For example in the experimental effort estimation models, the exponent is often relatively close to 1.0. This deviation from 1.0 might be due to some non-linear function, but it might be caused as well by some errors in the input parameters to the model. Consequently, the software effort could be characterized as an increasing linear function of the size of the projects, such as in Figures 6-6 and 6-7.

In Figure 6-6, it is clearly observed that a number of projects have an effort cost lower than that predicted by the model, while there are also quite a few projects with an effort cost higher than that predicted by the model. This model is, of course, based on a single independent variable, namely, the functional size; it cannot be realistically expected that this variable would by itself be sufficient to produce a perfect estimate without taking into consideration the large number of other independent variables (e.g. associated NFRs).

Of course, one might think of a number of other variables that can impact project effort, each having its own specific impact. The combination of the impact of these other independent variables will lead to an effort estimation number (that is, a number of person/hours) which may be lower or higher than the effort predicted by the regression line of a model with a single independent variable.

This is illustrated next with a real data set [Max09] taken from PROMISE DATA repository-(Maxwell) where the project data from one of the biggest commercial banks in Finland was collected. In Figure 6-8, the circles point out some projects that have a large functional size (measured in ISO 20926 [ISO2092603] units: FPA- Unadjusted Function Points) with very little corresponding effort (measured in person-hours). In the same figure, the squares point out some projects that have relatively small functional size with high effort. This illustrates well that a number of other variables (NFRs in this case), in addition to size, must be taken into account to explain individual project effort.

In the next section, we discuss how we use the linear regression technique within our proposed solution to estimate the effort of the project based on both FRs and NFRs.

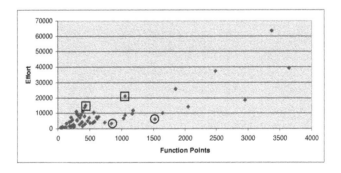

Figure 6-8: Visual Identification of Projects with a Smaller and Higher Unit Cost [Max09].

6.5.2 The solution proposal: Effort estimation model

The proposed process of measuring the effort of a project is carried out in 12 steps described below. In this process, Steps 1 and 2 are preparatory, Steps 3 and 4 are to treat elements of *class A*, Steps 5, 6, 7, 8 and 9 are concerned with *class B* elements, Step 10 treats *class C*, and Steps 11 and 12 treat *class D*. Figure 6-9 maps the described classes to the participating concepts from the NFRs Ontology. The steps of the proposed process are as follows:

Step 1 [FRs to COSMIC]: As suggested by the COSMIC method [ISO1976103], each FR is further refined into a sequence of subprocesses which are mapped to the COSMIC data movements: READ, WRITE, ENTRY and EXIT.

Step 2 [Ontology]: The proposed ontology view (Figure 6-4) is instantiated using the set of (i) the captured FRs, (ii) their mapped elements (e.g. tasks), and (iii) NFRs which are further refined through the decomposition and operationalization relations. The NFR's association relations with the association points are clearly captured.

Step 3 [Unadjusted Functional Size per functional process]: As proposed in the NFSM method in section 6.4, for each operationalization refined in Step 2 **AND** which corresponds to functions/operations; the functional size is calculated using the COSMIC method. (That includes mapping the operationalization into a sequence of COSMIC data movements). For each functionality-derived subprocesses, if the subprocesses is participating in *isAssociatingNfrTo* relation with an association point that participates in a *hasAssociationPoint* with an operationalization which correspond to a function/operation, then the functional size of the subprocesses is recalculated to add the extra size of the associated operationalization. It is important to notice that the functional size for an operationalization corresponding to a function/operation is to be considered more than once only if it operates on a different data group through its associations. This means, any duplicated pair of (operationalization , data group) will be considered only once.

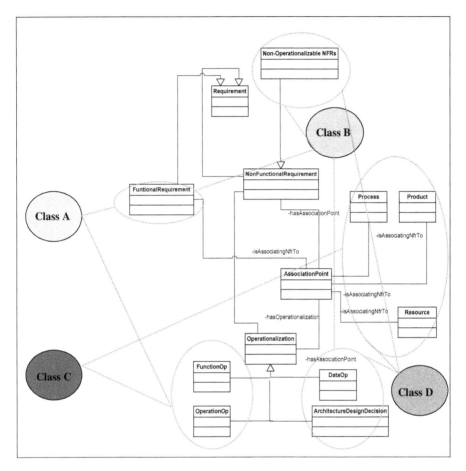

Figure 6-9: Mapping of the NFRs Concepts to the Steps of Measuring the Effort.

Step 4 [Unadjusted Functional Size per Requirement]: For each functional requirement, the functional size values of all subprocesses calculated in Step 3 are summed up. At this point, we generate the unadjusted functional size of FRs.

Step 5 [Ranking associations of Class B NFRs/Operationalizations]: For each identified association with elements of Class B NFRs / operationalizations, the association has further to be ranked on a 3-values scale [-, 0, +]. The first category, labeled with "-", indicates basically that the associated NFR / operationalization reduces the effort of building the functionality. The second category, referred to as to "o", indicates the absence of the impact of the associated NFR / operationalization on the effort for building the functionality. The third category, labeled with "+", means that the associated NFR / operationalization increases the effort of building the functionality.

As a future work, standardized definitions of the proposed scale will be required to improve repeatability of the classification for each category. This would ensure that the classification would be repeatable and reproducible across measures and across projects.

Step 6 [Initial Requirements Effort Estimation Model]: In this step, we build an initial "requirement" effort estimation model using a linear regression technique as described in section 6.5.1. As practitioners recommend [Mcco6], an estimation model is typically built with data from previous projects' FRs which have been delivered. From such a data set, an estimation model can be obtained through a linear regression model which basically builds the line that best represents the set of "requirements" in terms of effort (in person-hours) with respect to corresponding requirement functional size (in terms of CFP).

Step 7 [Unadjusted Effort per Requirement]: For each functionality, we map its unadjusted functional size calculated at step 4 to an unadjusted effort value on the regression line. At this point, we generate the unadjusted effort for the FR.

Step 8 [Adjusted Effort per Requirement]: For each functionality, its unadjusted effort value obtained at Step 7 is readjusted to take into account the associations with NFRs / Operationalizations of Class B. In the dataset, all requirements which lie precisely on the regression line of the initial estimation would correspond to requirements with all associated NFRs / operationalizations from step 5 (class B NFRs / operationalizations) being ranked as "o". That is, the regression line is interpreted as the line corresponding to the expected category with the dependent variable "effort" depends only on the size of the functionality. In the dataset, all the requirements with "increasing" effect on the effort, that is requirements with the maximum effort above the regression line and along the functional size axis, would correspond to requirements with all NFRs / operationalizations from Step 5 being classified in the "+" in the 3-values scale. In the dataset, all the requirements with "reduction" effect on the effort, that is requirements with the minimum effort below the regression line and along the functional size axis, would correspond to requirements with all NFRs / operationalizations from Step 5 being in the "-" category in the 3-values scale.

A graphical analysis on the obtained regression model can be carried out to identify both the max and min values on the graph; from there we can select a representative point along the vertical line at the corresponding functional size of the FR based on the classification of the NFRs / operationalizations done at Step 5. For example, if 50% of the NFRs / operationalizations have been rated "+", while the other 50% have been rated with "o" then we adjust the unadjusted effort by selecting the midpoint between the regression line and the max value: (Model value + max value) /2. At this point, we have an adjusted effort value for the FR.

We make a note here that this estimation approach does not attempt to model the individual effort relationship for each one of the associated NFR. However, it will use the information about these associated NFRs and the data from a historical dataset to graphically position the requirement to be estimated, in terms of required effort, somewhere between the minimum and the maximum effort for specific functional size in a dataset as a function of the set of NFRs.

Step 9 [Adjusted Functional Size per Requirement]: The adjusted effort value from Step 8 is projected across the regression line (inverse function) to get the adjusted functional size for the FR.

Step 10 [Unadjusted Functional Size per Project]: The total functional size values for all FRs from Step 9 are summed up.

Operationalizations which correspond to functions/operations and are associated to the whole product, process or resources, are to have their functional size calculated using the COSMIC method and directly added to the total calculated. Again, it is important to notice that the functional size for an operationalization corresponding to a function/operation is to be considered more than once only if it is operated on a different datagroup through its associations. In other words, any duplicated pair of (operationalization, datagroup) will be considered only once. At this step, we generate the unadjusted functional size of the whole project.

Step 11 [Initial Project Effort Estimation Model]: Similarly to what we did in Steps 6 and 7, Step 11 is about building an initial "project" effort estimation model using the regression technique. This time, we build the estimation effort model for the unadjusted functional size of the project, while in Step 6 we were doing this for the FR level. We then map the value obtained in step 10 across the regression line.

Step 12 [Adjusted Project Effort]: We adjust the total number obtained in Step 11 (namely, the unadjusted effort of the whole project) to take into account the associated NFRs/operationalizations from *class D* in a similar way as we did in Step 8. At this point, we generate the adjusted effort value for the project level.

The above described approach is illustrated next through a case study.

6.6 The Case Study

We have conducted an evaluation case study to illustrate our solution proposal. The goal of our study was to analyze the proposed effort estimation method with the purpose of evaluating its ability to predict the effort in the context of project of the undergraduate students in their third year of studies enrolled in the 2009 "Software Measurement" and "Software Project" software engineering courses at Concordia University, Montreal, Canada (see Chapter 3, Section 3.3.2). The project was described within 39 FRs with total initial measured functional size of 137 CFP (that is without considering the impact of the NFRs). The described ontology has been instantiated using the set of requirements extracted from the vision document and the use-case specifications. Eight NFRs have been captured. They have been all listed with their impact evaluations on their association points in Table 6-17. The listed NFRs are of type quality with exception of NFR7 which is an operating constraint.

Table 6-17: NFRs from IEEE-Montreal Project.

#	NFR/ OPERATIONALIZATION	DECOM-POSED FROM	ASSOC-IATED TO	IMP-ACT
NFR_1	The system should maintain provided services with high security when required.	-	System	+
NFR_2	The system should be available most of the time.	Security (NFR1)	System	+
NFR_3	The system should provide its functionalities with high confidentiality when it is required.	Security (NFR1)	All FRs but search	
NFR_4	The website should be easy to maintain by non expert users with no requiring for a third party interaction or costs for updates.		System	+
NFR_5	All technologies must be portable between Windows Linux and Mac platforms.		System	o

NFR[6]	Better and Easier Usability for the IEEE website.		System	+
NFR[7]	The system has a processing and data storage element. This part of the system will reside on the main IEEE computer and communicate with other IEEE systems.		System	+
NFR[8]	The system should be easy to modify (add new themes, blocks, menus, taxonomies, terms, columns, extend functionality, etc.).	Maintaina bility (NFR4)	Content Managem ent Functiona lity	+

Because NFR[1] and NFR[4] are not atomic, then they are not considered directly in the assessment of the effort. Among the specified NFRs in Table 6-17, only NFR[3] has been operationalized through functions which allow the creation and assignment of privileged access to the users. Basically, the new site must recognize several privilege/responsibility types for users and allow new user types to be added without re-coding. Table 6-18 lists the functionalities which operationalize NFR[3] along with their calculated functional size using the COSMIC method. These operationalizations would always operate on the same dataset regardless of the association points they are associated to. Thus, the functional size would be calculated only once.

Table 6-18: Operationalizations for NFR[3] (IEEE-Montreal Project).

OPERATIONALIZATION	FUNCTIONAL SIZE (CFP)
Get_Privileged_Access	6
Assign_User_Roles	6
Create_Role	6
Update_Role	6
Delete_Role	6
Release_Privileged_Access	6

Total size of the 6 operationalizations	36 CFP

The initial estimation model for requirements effort was based on the functional size for the requirements, and was built using the linear regression technique. For 59 developed requirements from 6 previous projects, the below regression model based on functional size was obtained. The projects were developed and completed by students in their third year of studies enrolled in the "Software Project" undergraduate course at Concordia University in 2008.

$$\text{Effort} = 2.34 * (\text{Functional Size}) + 4.24$$
$$\text{With Correlation Coefficient: } r = 0.734$$

The line in Figure 6-10 presents the above equation. That is, for a requirement with all associated NFRs having an average impact (classified in the "0" category"), the effort should be mapped to a point on this line. On the other hand, for a requirement with most associated NFRs classified in the "+" category, the effort should be mapped to a point above the regression line and below the point representing the highest possible effort: 192.25 person-hours.

Similarly, for a requirement with most associated NFRs classified in the "-" category, the effort should be mapped to a point below the regression line and above the point representing the lowest possible effort: 4.5 person-hours.

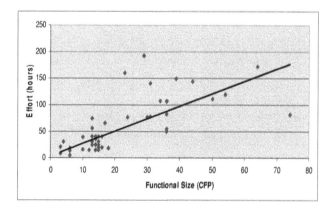

Figure 6-10: A Regression Model for Functional Requirements from Previously Completed Projects: Requirement Level.

We make the note that while the *content management* functionality is measured initially to have functional size of 30 CFP, NFR_8 is associated to *content management* and NFR_8 is operationalized through some design and architectural decisions and thus measuring its functional size is not possible. The impact of NFR_8 on its associated functionality is classified as '+'. Thus, the functional size of *content management* has to be adjusted to somewhere above the regression model estimate and below the point that corresponds to the highest impact of NFRs (NFR_8 is impacting *content management* in a moderate way not to bring the effort all the way to the highest effort). The best option would be the midpoint between the regression line and the highest effort.

The initial effort estimate for *content management* based on the above regression model without the impact of the maintainability NFR is:

Unadjusted Effort (*content management*) = 2.34 * (30) + 4.24 = 74.44 person-hours

The effort corresponding to the highest impact of NFRs at a requirement with a functional size of 30 CFP is: 192.25 person-hours

The midpoint between these two values is chosen to be the effort for the *content management*, thus the effort of *content management* is readjusted to be:

Adjusted Effort (*content management*) = (74.44 + 192.25) / 2 = 133.35 person-hours

With a new effort value for *content management*, its corresponding functional size has been readjusted. We calculate the functional size for *content management* based on the newly added effort:

133.35 = 2.34 * (Functional Size) + 4.24

Adjusted_Functional Size = (133.35 − 4.24) / 2.34 = 55.18 CFP.

The total functional size for all FRs is recalculated at this point: 137 + (55.18 − 30) + 36= 198.18 CFP.

The same procedure is repeated on the project level. The regression model obtained based on previously completed projects is the following one:

Effort = 1.24 * (Functional Size) + 382.6

With Correlation coefficient: 0.49

The line in Figure 6-11 presents the above formula. This line is bounded by two points, the first of which corresponds to the minimal effort: 412 person-hours and the second one corresponds to the max efforts: 783.75 person-hours

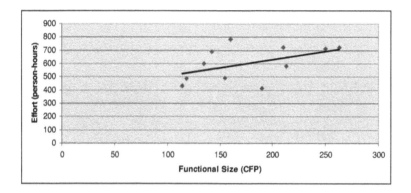

Figure 6-11: A Regression Model for Previously Completed Projects: Project Level

Based on the calculated functional size for all requirements, the initial effort for building the project is calculated as:

Unadjusted Effort (project) = 1.24 * (198.18) + 382.6= 628.34 person-hours.
Now, to adjust the effort, we should consider the effect of the remaining NFRs; that is NFR_2, NFR_5, NFR_6 and NFR_7.
Because 3 out of these 4 NFRs associated to the projects presented in Table 5-17, are deemed high impact NFRs, the total effort for the project should be readjusted to fall on a higher point above the regression line. Based on expert's judgment, the best representative point on the functional size axis is 75% above the regression line and 25% below the max value.
Thus, the total effort of the software project with all associated NFRs is calculated to be:
(((628.34+ 783.75) / 2) + 783.75) /2= 744.9 person-hours.
In order to evaluate our approach in comparison with the traditional practice of not considering the impact of NFRs in estimating the effort, we have generated the Magnitude Relative Error (MRE) for the captured actual effort and calculated results from our approach. Then we have established a comparison among the MREs value having our calculated effort value as an input

against having the value of the effort calculated without considering the impact of NFRs. The MRE is calculated through the below formula below:

MRE (Project) = ABS ((Actual Effort − Estimated Effort) / Actual Effort)

The actual reported effort for the IEEE-website project was: 820.75 person-hours. The MRE for the captured actual effort and calculated results from our approach is:
$$ABS ((820.75 − 744.9) / 820.75) = 9.24 \%$$
If we would have chosen not to follow our approach and, instead, to consider only the impact of the FRs, then with 137 CFP as an initial functional size, the estimated effort would have been:
$$Effort = 1.24 * (137) + 382.6 = 552.48 \text{ person-hours}$$
The MRE for the captured actual effort and calculated results without considering the impact of NFRs:
$$ABS ((820.75 − 552.48) / 820.75) = 32.59 \%$$
This is a 23.35% improvement in the effort estimation.

6.6 Conclusion

The effort estimation approach presented in this chapter aims at improving the predictive quality of the software industry's effort estimation models. This chapter demonstrated the feasibility of the proposed approach on a case study. To the best of our knowledge, the software industry lacks quantitative effort estimation methods for NFRs, and would certainly benefit from the precise and objective size measurement and effort estimation approach proposed in this chapter.

On the other hand, the proposed effort estimation model is expected to be adopted relatively easier in those organiozations who have already made experiences with quantitative mamangement of software projects. We consider the following prerequisites instrumental to the adoption: (1) experience with a FP-like approach, preferably COSMIC, (2) culture of measurement-oriented thinking of software processes, (3) Access to a historical dataset which is collected from completed projects and implemented requirements; and it is sufficient to build the required regression model for both the requirements and the project levels and (4) Having both FRs and NFRs captured and well-documented.

Our approach has similarity with other regression-based estimation approaches in that the analysts make a number of simplifying assumptions when using this type of approaches. Such assumptions might pose threats to various extents to the validity of the final results [Rei90]. For example, an analyst can base his/her choice of '-/o/+' ratings on his/her own experience in implementing specific NFRs in a project in an organization. While for some NFRs, as reusability, it might be possible for the analyst to find some published research on what levels of reuse are achievable in a specific type of project and what is the effort associated with this, for other NFRs the analyst might set up the ratings in a way that - clearly, could be subjective. However, it is our understanding that at this early stage of research on NFR-based effort estimation, this design choice is the only possible way to go. We plan, in the future, a deeper research on the topic of evaluating the validity of our solution proposal in various settings, expecting that new knowledge will help refine our approach.

Further discussion on the future work is presented in the next chapter.

Chapter VII: Conclusion and Future Work

> "Not to be absolutely certain is, I think, one of the essential things in rationality."
> Bertrand Russell (1872 - 1970)

7.1 Conclusion

The tendency for NFRs to have a wide-ranging impact on a software system, the strong interdependencies among them, and the NFR tradeoffs; all challenge current software modeling methods. As a result, how to integrate NFRs and FRs into a coherent requirements engineering process is a problem which has only been partially solved. However, the increasing trend to develop complex software systems has highlighted the urgent need to consider NFRs as an integral part of software system development.

In this book, we contribute towards achieving the overall goal of managing the attainable scope and the changes of NFRs. We achieve that through:

1. Building a formal metamodel for FRs, NFRs and their relations which was implemented as the proposed NFRs ontology.

2. Implementing change management mechanism for tracing the impact of NFR on other constructs in the formal metamodel and the corresponding NFRs Ontology and vice versa.

3. Proposing a novel approach to the NFRs scope management and early requirements-based effort estimation based on the NFR formal metamodel and the corresponding ontology.

One of the advantages of our approach is that it forces systems analysts to understand the relationships that exist within and across NFRs in the various phases of development right from the requirements inception phase till the implementation and testing phases.

Benefits which arise by blending our research results with existing industry practice can further make an enhancement of their expertise about requirements engineering and software architectures with respect to NFRs. Our research will help to deliver ready-to-use methods that could be easily applied in consulting interventions at clients' sites. For example a validated traceability approach will allow the industry to improve the synergies among their requirements engineering, architectural design, implementation and testing processes. To the best of our knowledge, the software industry lacks quantitative effort estimation methods for NFRs, and would certainly benefit from the precise and systematic proposed model presented in chapter 6.

Table 7-1 revisits the research questions we discussed in Chapter 3 and links each question to the corresponding section in this book in which the question is addressed.

Table 7-1: Linking Research Questions to their Corresponding Answers.

Research Question	Link to the Answer
Q1- What is a NFR?	Sections 4.4.1 and 4.5.1
Q2-What are the types of NFRs? How can they be categorized?	Section 4.5.2.1
Q3- How does NFR interact with FRs and their refinements during the software development process?	Section 4.5.1
Q4- How does one NFR interact with other NFRs?	Sections 4.5.2.2, 4.5.2.3 and 4.5.2.4
Q5- What are the concepts and relationships which characterize the interactions referred to in Q3 and Q4?	Section 4.5
Q6: What traceability mechanisms are used in theory and practice to support requirements engineering and architectural design decisions for NFRs? What complexity aspects of NFRs are accounted for in current requirements engineering and architectural design decision-making processes?	Section 5.2
Q7: What are the critical areas requiring traceability attention when dealing with change management of NFRs? How are these areas mapped to the concepts and relationships defined in the NFRs Ontology?	Sections 5.3 and 5.4
Q8: What is the impact of NFRs on the total effort for building and maintaining the software project?	Section 6.3
Q9: In which ways are NFRs treated in current theoretical and practical effort estimation models?	Section 6.3
Q10: How to improve the existing practice of early estimation for the effort taking into account the impact of NFRs?	Sections 6.4, 6.5 and 6.6

Table 7-2 restates the applicability of the approaches resulting from this research with steps towards deploying the approach in practice. In addition, it provides the links to the corresponding sections of evaluation in which the reader can refer to the demonstration on how to apply the proposed approach.

In this book, we presented the illustration and the evaluation through settings from three case studies. Having different case studies design usually offer greater validity for the work [ESSD07]. The following items summarize our findings from the interaction with the selected case studies:

1.   There is no consensus on how to specify NFRs. These requirements can be listed under "Non-Functional Requirements", "Usability Requirements" or "Technical Requirements" as in the IEEE Montreal-website case study, "Solution Requirements"as in Nokia Mobile Email Application case study or even under "Configuration Requirements" as in the SAP case study. In this book, we define NFR as an umbrella term to cover all those requirements which are not explicitly defined as functional.

2.   The "perspective" of the requirement is a major dimension to consider when dealing with NFRs. What can be listed as a FR from certain perspective may be considered as NFR from another.

3.   Type of the project has a major influence on the type of NFRs which are most likely to be demanded. For example, in Nokia Mobile Email application case study, in order to optimize the user experience for devices with limitations (e.g. screen size, memory, processing speed) and wireless networks with constrained bandwidth, performance is a high-priority NFR. On othe other hand, for web applications that have an informative objectives, usability is a high-priority NFR. The link between the type of the project and the demanded NFRs is a subject of future investigation.

4.   We acknowledge that using the students for research studies poses further challenge in terms of balancing different objectives when conducting empirical or observational studies as part of an academic course. In order to minimize the effect of the potential challenge, the research's objectives were clearly connected to educational goals. Mandatory participation may affect the results, but optional participation is not necessarily better. We prompted the invitation for participation as an optional bonus assignment. The students were then given the necessary training to conduct the tasks of the assignment and multuiple Q/A sessions were set to address the raised concerns.

Table 7-2: Applicability of Approaches Resulting from this Thesis.

Phase	Applicability	Steps towards deploying in practice	Evaluation
Phase 1	Improving the NFRs specification process.	Follow the steps towards NFRs Instantation (Figure 4-17).	Section 4.7
Phase 2	Improving the testing practices for NFR on deployed software using the proposed traceability mechanism.	1- Transform the NFRs Ontology into corresponding relational-model based representation. 2- Upon a change request, identify the potentially impacted areas along with their specifications and refinements. 3- Execute the corresponding query. 4- Once the retrival algorithm has returned a set of potentially impacted requirements / elements filter the retrieved requirements/elements to remove any non-relevant ones. 6- A decision on any accepted change in any of the retrieved data should be recorded in the corresponding relations.	Section 5.6
Phase 3	Better prediction for the effort of building the software project taking the impact of NFRs into consideration.	1- Measure the functional size of the operationalizations in isolation from their relations; 2- Refer to the instantiated NFRs Ontology for the clear specification on NFRs relations and specifications. 3- Adjust the functional size of the captured functionalities and the total project using the measurement from (1) and the specification of NFR's relations from (2). 4- When the size of the operationalizations cannot be measured OR the NFRs	Section 6.6

		cannot be refined into design solutions (unoperationalized NFRs), we then consider the impact of these operationalizations and "unoperationalized NFRs" on the size of functionalities and the effort of building the project through an estimation models based on regression techniques.	

This work is multidisciplinary in nature, which opened multiple avenues of future work that we could effectively pursue. Our main interests are discussed in the following sections categorized by the identified 'purpose' from Chapter 1.

7.2 Future Work on Characterizing NFRs

Clearly, the evaluation of the acceptance and the accuracy of the NFRs Ontology, as such, ultimately rely upon its application by the research community. The author of this book and the scientific supervisors are hoping to soon benefit from interaction with a number of interested parties in this topic. In particular, we plan to explore the way in which NFRs Ontology could be further leveraged in more complex requirements specification scenarios in real-life settings. In order to ground the concept further, we plan to develop tools to leverage the benefits of ontology for NFRs and evaluate our results against scenarios designed to test the capabilities of the ontology (See Section 4.3.1). We are also planning to collaborate with industrial partners such as NOKIA office in Montreal to deploy and instantiate the NFRs Ontology in their upcoming projects.

We are also working closely with the Computational Linguistic research team at Concordia University on a project that aims at automating the instantiation process for the NFRs Ontology from sets of requirements specification documents to be used as an input. The automation of the NFRs instantiation process will contribute towards better acceptance for the proposed ontology in the industrial firm.

In addition, we will investigate further to which degree having the NFRs Ontology adopted in the requirements engineering activities guarantees the compliance of the final product with the captured NFRs.

On other hand, we started working on extending the ontology to establish a formal methodology to resolve the conflict between NFRs (Chapter 4, Section 4.5.2.4) with minimal contribution from stakeholders. The background context for this work is provided by other authors' previously published research, namely [Lee96] who developed a formal model for the WinWin requirements engineering process called the "Problem Space View". We have deployed this process to evaluate its applicability in a context of a conflict which may rise in case of a large size of demanded software vs. limited available effort (limited human resources). This model was chosen for our investigation because of its formal mathematical basis, which allows for automation of the process and thus for objectively assessing NFR risk management. The model defines a win condition as a constraint on the space R of all requirement specifications. R consists of a set of functional, infrastructure, and quality attribute specifications. In the model, a conflict is defined as a set of win conditions, the win regions of which have an empty intersection (the bottom space in Figure 7-1). Lee maintained that the conflict could be resolved by expanding stakeholders' win condition area (called "satisfactory area"). In [In98], the author proposed a theory for resolving conflicts by creating options through added dimensions. The conflict in the n dimension space (the bottom space in Figure 7-1) can be resolved in the space of the $n+1^{st}$ dimension (see the top space in Figure 7-1) by expanding stakeholders' win conditions due to the added dimension (called "option strategy").

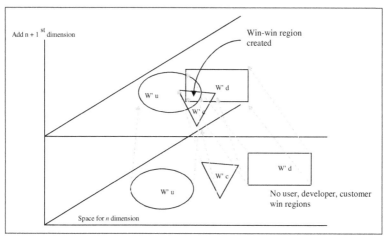

Figure 7-1: Conflict Resolution through Added Dimensions.

An example of a conflict situation in n-dimensional space is shown in Figure 7-2. The numbers in the example are for purposes of illustration. In this example, the user's win condition, W(U)1, consists of more than 15 functions, but the customer's win condition, W(C)1, is that the effort should be less than 28 person-months [pm]. The developer's win condition, W(D)1, is a reasonable expectation of work and reward (i.e. not too much work, but enough income) as estimated by an effort estimation model such as COCOMO. In the example, it is assumed for simplicity that each function has a function size of 30 CFP and requires 2 [pm]. Figure 7-2 shows that there is no WinWin area to satisfy all stakeholders' constraints, because the total functional size for a project implementing the 15 functions is estimated to be 450 CFP, and thus the total effort is 30 [pm].

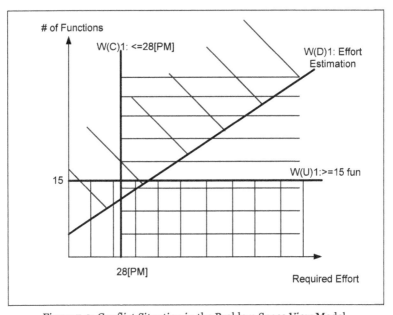

Figure 7-2: Conflict Situation in the Problem Space View Model.

The following steps, which were used to solve the decision problem with constraints, represent the effort conflict situation more specifically:

1. Define an objective:
   • Find the WinWin region (i.e. the region that satisfies all constraint win conditions)
2. Define the decision variables:

•x1: Effort

•x2: # of functions

3. Define the constraints according to each win condition:

•g1(x1, x2): x1 <= 28 [pm]

•g2(x1, x2): x2 >= 15

•g3(x1, x2): x1 <= 2[pm] * x2 (= our assumption for simplicity)

4. Identify the WinWin region (the satisfactory area for all stakeholders):

•No WinWin region (i.e. conflict)

5. Identify the WinWin point (the most satisfactory point for all stakeholders within the WinWin region), if the WinWin region exists.

Figure 7-3 shows an example of resolution of the effort conflict situation presented above. The effort conflict situation shown in Figure 7-2 can be represented in the bottom space in Figure 7-3. The effort conflict can be resolved by creating an option, namely, that of reusing existing software assets which perform some of the 15 functions, which is generated by an added dimension, "reuse of software assets (%)". The reuse of software assets can reduce the effort needed for the current phase without reducing the number of functions the user wants to implement. This conflict resolution situation is shown in the upper part of Figure 7-3. One of the assumptions, for simplicity, is that complete reuse saves the total effort. Thus, reusing 3 functions (20% of 15 functions) saves 6 [pm] and reduces the total effort to 24 [pm].

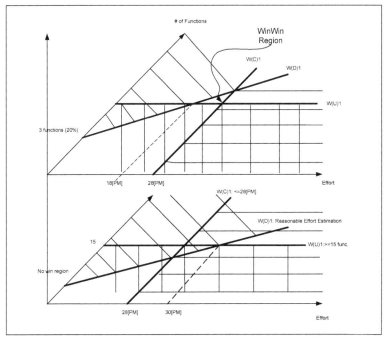

Figure 7-3: An Example of Cost Conflict Resolution through an Added Dimension.

Using the steps to represent cost conflicts, the conflict resolution process by option creation through an added dimension can also be represented more specifically by means of the following steps:

1. Define an objective:
    •Find the WinWin region
2. Define the decision variables:
    •x1: Effort
    •x2: # of functions
3. Define constraints:
    •g1(x1, x2): x1 <= 28 [pm]
    •g2(x1, x2): x2 >= 15
    •g3(x1, x2): x1 <= 2 [pm] * x2
4. If there is no WinWin area (i.e. conflict), add an additional dimension; for example,

$x3 (= \#$ functions covered by reuse of software assets):

- $\bullet g1(x1, x2, x3): x1 <= 28 \text{ [pm]}$
- $\bullet g2(x1, x2, x3): x2 >= 15$
- $\bullet g3'(x1, x2, x3): x1 <= 2 \text{ [pm]} * (x2 - x3)$

5. Identify the WinWin region (the satisfactory area for all stakeholders):

- $\bullet x1 <= 28 \text{ [pm]}; x2 <= 15; 2 <= x3 <= 3$ (the blank area in Figure 4)

6. Identify the WinWin value (the most satisfactory point for all stakeholders within the WinWin region), if the WinWin region exists.

Clearly, the proposed dimensions depend on the type of conflicts. Typically, there are proposed dimensions for a specific type of conflict. For example, reducing/deferring functionality, reducing/deferring quality, relaxing schedule constraints, improving personnel capability, improving tools and platform, reusing software assets, and increasing budget can all be viable means of resolving cost conflicts. One remaining challenge here is conflicts that may arise in the large requirement model which we are unable to identify automatically; in other words, scalability is yet to be determined through larger cases studies from the real world.

7.3 Future Work on NFRs Traceability

Change management would require not only a mechanical tracing of the effects of change, but also a reasoned approach to gauging the consistency of the changes within the traceability model. Due to the complexity of the NFRs relations in the traceability model, a change analysis mechanism is required to ensure the consistency of the proposed changes before they are authorized. Our future work includes the development of consistency rules based on the formal presentation of the FR and NFR hierarchies and their relations, rules which will be automatically checked before a change is authorized.

In addition, we plan to remedy further evaluation for the traceability mechanism by extending its applicability beyond the testing activities (e.g. requirements review activities, project's extension.) This will be done by applying empirical research methods, specifically case studies and experiments.

We will also consider the mapping of the Datalog expressions into SPARQL Protocol and RDF Language (SPARQL) which is an RDF query language. SPARQL was standardized by the RDF Data Access Working Group (DAWG) of the World Wide Web Consortium, and is considered a key semantic web technology. SPARQL, which became an official W3C recommendation in

2008, allows for a query to consist of triple patterns, conjunctions, and optional patterns. Implementing the traceability queries with SPARQL blends phases 1 and 2 of this research in a more consistent fashion.

7.4 Future Work on Effort Estimation considering the impact of NFRs

As the author of this book is working in a company interested in the effort estimation approach, he and his supervisors plan to investigate further the impact of interactivity relation on the effort estimation. The effect of additional independent variables such as experience and project difficulty will be combined then into in a multiplicative regression model, which may improve significantly the quality of the project effort estimation model. In addition, we plan on considering the automation for the effort estimation process presented in chapter 6. We also plan on extending the effort estimation model to the "cost" range (e.g. determine how the size of NFRs impacts the total cost).

References

[ABH05] Anda, B., Benestad, H.C., & Hove, S.E. (2005). A Multiple-Case Study Of Effort Estimation Based On Use Case Points, *In ISESE 2005 (Fourth International Symposium On Empirical Software Engineering)*, IEEE Computer Society, Noosa, Australia, November 17-18, (pp. 407- 416).

[Abr09] Abran, A. (2009). *Software Estimation Models: Can You Trust Them.*

[Abr99] Abran, A. (1999). COSMIC FFP 2.0: An Implementation of COSMIC functional size measurement concepts. *In Proceedings of the 2nd European Software Measurement Conference* (FESMA'99), (Oct. 7), Amsterdam.

[ACK05] Al-Kilidar, H., Cox, K., & Kitchenham, B. (2005). The use and usefulness of the ISO/IEC 9126 quality standard, *2005 International Symposium on Empirical Software Engineering,* (pp. 126- 132).

[ADOSS03] Abran, A., Desharnais, J. M., Oligny, S., St-Pierre, D., & Symons, C. (2003). COSMIC FFP – Measurement Manual (COSMIC implementation guide to ISO/IEC 19761:2003), École de technologie supérieure – Université du Québec, Montréal, Canada.

[AG83] Albrecht, A. J., & Gaffney J. E. (1983). Software function, source lines of code, and development effort prediction: A software science validation, *IEEE Transactions Software Engineering,* 9(6), (pp. 639– 648).

[Alb79] Albrecht, A. J. (1979). Measuring application development productivity, *In Proceedings of the IBM Applications Development Symposium*, Monterey, California, (pp. 83– 92).

[Alb84] Albrecht, A. J. (1984). *AD/M Productivity Measurement and Estimate Validation*, IBM Corporate Information Systems, IBM Corp., Purchase, NY.

[AMBR02] Araujo, J., Moreira, A., Brito, I., & Rashid, A. (2002). Aspect-Oriented Requirements With UML, *Workshop on Aspect-Oriented Modeling with UML (held with UML 2002,* Dresden, Germany.

[ANRS06] Aizenbud-Reshef, N., Nolan, B.T., Rubin, J., & Shaham-Gafni, Y. (2006). Model Traceability, *IBM System Journal*, 45(3), (pp. 515- 526).

[Ant97] Antón, A. (1997). *Goal Identification and Refinement in the Specification of Information Systems*, Ph.D. Thesis, Georgia Institute of Technology.

[AOA04] Abran, A., Ormandjieva, O., & Abu Talib, M. (2004). Information Theory-Based Functional Complexity Measures and Functional Size With COSMIC-FFP, *Proceedings Of The 14th International Workshop On Software Measurement (Iwsm2004)*, Germany.

[AR94] Abran, A., & Robillard, P. N. (1994). Function Points: A Study Of Their Measurement Processes And Scale Transformations, *Journal Of Systems And Software,* 25(2), (pp. 171- 184).

[ASDL07] Al Balushi, T. H., Sampaio, P. R., Dabhi, D., & Loulopoulos, P. (2007). ElicitO: A Quality Ontology-Guided NFR Elicitation Tool, *Proceeding Of REFSQ 2007, Requirements Engineering: Foundations for Software Quality,* Trondheim, Norway, (pp. 306- 319).

[ASHKW06] Ankolekar, A., Sycara, K., Herbsleb, J., Kraut, R., & Welty, C. (2006). Supporting Online Problem-solving Communities with the Semantic Web. *In Proceeding of the 15th International Conference on WWW,* (pp. 575–584).

[ASM01] Angelis, L., Stamelos, I., & Morisio, M. (2001). Building A Software Cost Estimation Model Based On Categorical Data, *In Proceedings of the 7th international Symposium on Software Metrics, METRICS, IEEE Computer Society,* Washington, DC.

[ASMD98] Abran, A., St-Pierre, D., Maya, M., & Desharnais, J. M. (1998). Full function points for embedded and real-time software, *In Proceedings of the UKSMA Fall Conference,* London, UK.

[BAB+00] Boehm, B., Abts, C., Brown, A., Chulani, S., Clark, B., Horowitz, E., Madachy, R., Reifer, D., & Steece, B. (2000). *Software cost estimation with COCOMO II* (with CD-ROM), Englewood Cliffs, NJ:Prentice-Hall, ISBN 0-13-026692-2.

[Bas96] Basili, V. R. (1996). The role of experimentation in software engineering: past, current, and future, *Proceedings of the 18th international conference on Software engineering,* Berlin, Germany, (pp. 442- 449).

[Bab85] Babcock, C. (1985). New Jersey Motorists in Software Jam, *Computerworld,* September, 30, (pp. 1- 6).

[BB99] Blair, L., & Blair, G. (1999). A Tool Suite to Support Aspect-Oriented Specification, *In Aspect Oriented Programming Workshop in Conjunction with the 13th European Conference on Object-Oriented Programming,* Lisbon, Portugal, (pp. 7– 10).

[BBL76] Boehm, B. W., Brown, J. R., & Lipow, M. (1976). Quantitative Evaluation of Software Quality, *In proceeding of the 2nd International Conference on Software Engineering,* San Francisco, CA, Long Branch, CA: IEEE Computer Society, (pp. 592- 605).

[BCAMRT06] Baniassad, E., Clements, P.C., Araujo, J., Moreira, A., Rashid, A., & Tekinerdogan, B. (2006). Discovering Early Aspects, *IEEE Software,* 23(1), (pp. 61- 70).

[BCK03] Bass, L., Clements, P., & Kazman, R. (2003). *Software Architecture in Practice,* Addison-Wesley, NY.

[BG06] Berenbach, B., & Gall, M. (2006). Toward a Unified Model for Requirements Engineering, *Proceedings of the IEEE international conference on Global Software Engineering,* (pp. 237 – 238).

[BHS03] Baader, F., Horrocks, I., & Sattler, U. (2003). Description logics as ontology languages for the semantic web, *in Lecture Notes in Artificial Intelligence, Springe*, http://www.cs.man.ac.uk/~horrocks/Publications/download/2003/BaHS03.pdf/

[BI96] Boehm, B., & In, H. (1996). Identifying Quality-Requirement Conflicts, *IEEE Software*, IEEE Computer Society Press, (pp. 25- 35).

[BKW03] Berry, D.M., Kazman, R., & Wieringa, R. (2003). Report on the Second International Workshop on From Software Architectures to Architectures (STRAW'03), *25th IEEE International Conference on Software Engineering*, IEEE Computer Science Press, (pp. 797- 798).

[BKWZ94] Banker, R., Kauffman, R. J., Wright, C., & Zweig, D. (1994). Automating output size and reuse metrics in a repository based computer aided software engineering (CASE) environment, *IEEE Transactions Software Engineering, 20* (3), (pp. 169– 187).

[BLF99] Breitman, K. K., Leite J. C. S. P., & Finkelstein, A. (1999). The World's Stage: A Survey on Requirements Engineering Using a Real-Life Case Study, *Journal of the Brazilian Computer Society*, 1(6), (pp. 13- 37).

[BM04] Brito, I., & Moreira, A. (2004). Integration the NFR Framework in a RE Model, *In Workshop on Early Aspects in Conjunction with 3rd International Conference on Aspect Oriented Software Development*, Lancaster, UK.

[Boe78] Boehm, B. (1978). *Characteristics of Software Quality*, North Holland Press.

[Boe81] Boehm, B. (1981). *Software engineering economics*, Englewood Cliffs, NJ:Prentice-Hall, ISBN 0-13-822122-7.

[BSA07] Blaauboer, F.A., Sikkel, K., & Aydin, M.N. (2007). Deciding to Adopt Requirements Traceability in Practice, *In Proceeding Of 19th International Conference on Advanced Information Systems Engineering (CAiSE'07)*, Springer Lecture Notes in Computer Science 4495, Norway, (pp. 294-308).

[BSH86] Basili, V. R., Selby, R. W. & Hutchens, D. H. (1986). Experimentation in Software Engineering, *IEEE Transactions on Software Engineering*, 12(7), (pp. 733- 743).

[BTV06] Berota, M., Troya, J. M., Vallecillo, A. (2006). Measuring the Usability of Software Components, Journals of Systems and Software, 79(3), (pp. 427 – 439).

[BWT85] Bowen, T. P., Wigle, G. B., & Tsai, J. T. (1985). Specification of Software Quality Attributes, Volume 2, *Software Quality Specification Guidebook*.

[CAFL98] Caldiera, G., Antoniol, G., Fiutem, R., & Lokan, C. (1998). Definition and experimental evaluation for object oriented systems, *In Proceedings of the 5th International Symposium on Software Metrics* (METRICS 98), Nov. 20–21, Bethesda MD, (pp. 167– 178).

[CC98] Copi, I. M., & Cohen, C. (1998), *Introduction to Logic*, 10th edition, Prentice Hall.

[CDDD03] Cooper, K., Dai, L., Deng, Y., & Dong, J. (2003). Towards an Aspect-Oriented Architectural Framework, *In 2nd International Workshopon Aspect-Oriented Requirements Engineering and Architecture Design (Early Aspects)*, Boston, MA.

[CE00] Czarnecki, K., & Eisenecker, U.W. (2000). *Generative Programming*, Addison-Wesley, Reading.

[CFM06] Coral, C., Francisco, R., & Mario, P. (2006). *Ontologies for Software Engineering and Software Technology,* Springer, Berlin, Heidelberg.

[CH06] Gonzalez-Perez, C., & Henderson-Sellers, B. (2006). An Ontology for Software Development Methodologies and Endeavours, Ontologies for Software Engineering and Software Technology, Springer, (pp.123– 151).

[CIMS04] Conte, M., Iorio, T., Meli, R., & Santillo, L. (2004). E&Q: An early and quick approach to functional size measurement methods, *In Proceedings of Software Measurement European Forum* (SMEF), Rome, Italy.

[CK94] Chidamber, S. R., & Kemerer, C. F. (1994). A Metrics Suite for Object Oriented Design, *IEEE Transactions on Software Engineering*, 20(6), (pp. 476- 493).

[CKK01] Clements, P., Kazman, R., & Klein, M. (2001). *Evaluating Software Architectures: Methods and Case Studies*, Addison-Wesley Professional, NY.

[CL01] Cysneiros, L. M., & Leite, J.C.S.P. (2001). Using UML to reflect Non-functional Requirements, *Proceedings of the 2001 conference of the Centre for Advanced Studies on Collaborative research*, (pp. 2- 17).

[Cle05] Cleland-Huang, J. (2005). Toward Improved Traceability of Non-Functional requirements, *Proceedings of the 3rd international workshop on Traceability in emerging forms of softwareengineering*, Long Beach, California, (pp. 14 – 19).

[CLN01] Cysneiros, L.M., Leite, J.C.S.P., & Neto, J.S.M. (2001). A Framework for Integrating Non-Functional Requirements into Conceptual Models, *Requirements Engineering Journal*, 6(2), (pp. 97-115).

[CNY95] Chung, L., Nixon, B.A., & Yu, E. (1995). Using Non-Functional Requirements to Systematically Support Change, *Proceedings of the Second IEEE International Symposium on Requirements Engineering*, York, U.K., (pp. 132 – 139).

[CNYM00] Chung, L., Nixon, B.A., Yu, E., & Mylopoulos, J. (2000). *Nonfunctional Requirements in Software Engineering*, Kluwer Academic Publishing.

[CS04] Constantinides, C., & Skotiniotis, T. (2004). Providing multidimensional decomposition in object-oriented analysis and design, The *IASTED International Conference on Software Engineering (SE 2004)*, Innsbruck, Austria.

[CSBBC05] Cleland-Huang, J., Settimi, R., BenKhadra, O., Berezhanskaya, E., & Christina, S. (2005). Goal Centric Traceability for Managing Non-Functional Requirements, *Proceedings of the 27th international conference on Software engineering*, (pp. 362 - 371).

[CWM02] Common Warehouse Metamodel (CWM) Specification. (2002). http://www.cwmforum.org

[Dan05] Daneva, M. (2005). Architecture Maturity and Requirements Process Maturity Do not Explain Each Other, *Workshop on Software Measurement, German-Canadian Society of Software Metrics*, Shaker Verlag, Aachen.

[Dav93] Davis, A. (1993). *Software Requirements: Objects, Functions and States*, Prentice Hall.

[Dem82] Demarco, T. (1982). *Controlling Software Projects*, Yourdon press, New York.

[DKPWO07] Daneva, M., Kassab, M., Ponisio, M. L., & Wieringa R., & Ormandjieva. O. (2007). Exploiting a Goal-Decomposition Technique to Prioritize Non-functional Requirements. *Proceedings of the 10th Workshop on Requirements Engineering WER 2007*, Toronto, Canada.

[DKVP03] Dorr, J., Kerkow, D., Von Knethen, A., & Peach, B. (2003). Eliciting Efficiency Requirements with Use Cases, *In Proceedings of the International Workshop on Requirements Engineering: Foundations of Software Quality (REFSQ'2003)*.

[DLS05] Dobson, G., Lock, R., & Sommerville, I. (2005). Quality of Service Requirement Specification using an Ontology, *Conference Proceedings 1st International Workshop on Service-Oriented Computing: Consequences for Engineering Requirements (SOCCER'05)*, Paris, France.

[DSD02] Dimitrov, E., Schmietendorf, A., & Dumke, R. (2002). UML-Based Performance Engineering Possibilities and Techniques, *IEEE Software*, 19(1), (pp. 74-83).

[EDBS04] Ebert, C., Dumke, R., Bundschuh, M., & Schmietendorf, A. (2004). *Best Practices in Software Measurement: How to use metrics to improve project and process performance*, Springer.

[EG04] Egyed, A., & Grunbacher, P. (2004). Identifying Requirements Conflicts and Cooperation: How Quality Attributes and Automated Traceability Can Help, *IEEE Software*, 21(6), (pp. 50- 58).

[ESSD07] Easterbrook, S. M., Singer, J., Storey, M, & Damian, D. (2007). Selecting Empirical Methods for Software Engineering Research. In *F. Shull and J. Singer (eds) Guide to Advanced Empirical Software Engineering*, Springer.

[FD96] Finkelstein, A., & Dowell, J. (1996). A Comedy of Errors: The London Ambulance Service Case Study, *proceedings of the 8th International Workshop Software Specifications and Design*, (pp. 2- 5).

[FE00] Finkelstein, A., & Emmerich, W. (2000). The Future of Requirements Management Tools, *In Information Systems in Public Administration and Law, G. Quirchmayr, R. Wagner and M. Wimmer (Eds.): Oesterreichische Computer Gesellschaft*.

[Fir03] Firesmith, D. G. (2003). Common concepts underlying safety, security, and survivability engineering, Technical Note CMU/SEI-2003-TN-033, Carnegie Mellon Software Engineering Institute.

[FISMA08] FISMA, FiSMA 1.1 Functional Size Measurement Method, ISO/IEC 29881, http://www.fisma.fi/wp-content/uploads/2008/07/fisma_fsmm_11_for_web.pdf

[For04] Forselius, P. (2004). *Finnish Software Measurement Association Functional Size,* Finnish Software Metrics Association, Finland.

[FP97] Fenton, N.E., & Pfleeger, S.L. (1997). *Software Metrics: A rigorous and Practical Approach*, International Thomson Computer Press.

[FTAS08] Feldt, R., Torkar, R., Angelis, L., & Samuelsson, M. (2008). Towards individualized software engineering: empirical studies should collect psychometrics, *In Proceedings of the 2008 international Workshop on Cooperative and Human Aspects of Software Engineering* (Leipzig, Germany, May 13 - 13, 2008), CHASE '08, ACM, New York, NY, (pp. 49-52).

[GD08] Gencel, C., & Demirors, O. (2008). Functional size measurement revisited, *ACM Transactions Software Engineering Methodol,* 17(3), (pp. 1-36).

[Gen08] Gencel, C. (2008). How to use COSMIC Functional Size in Effort Estimation Models, *In the Proceeding Of Mensura/IWSM/Metrikon 2008 conference, LNCS 2008.*

[GF94] Gotel, O., & Finkelstein, A. (1994). An Analysis of the Requirements Traceability Problem, *Proceeding First International Conference Requirements Engineering*, Colorado, U.S.A, (pp. 94-101).

[GGKH03] Gardner, T., Griffin, C., Koehler, J., & Hauser, R. (2003). A review of OMG MOF 2.0 Query/Views/Transformations submissions and recommendations towards the final standard, *In 1st International Workshop on Metamodeling for MDA*, York, UK.

[GKM08] Gasevic, D., Kaviani, N., & Milanovic, M. (2008). Ontologies and Software Engineering, *In Staab, S. & Studer, R. (Eds.) - Handbook on Ontologies, Springer.*

[Gli05] Glinz, M. (2005). Rethinking the Notion of Non-Functional Requirements, *Proceeding of the 3rd World Congress for Software Quality*, Munich, Germany.

[Gli07] Glinz, M. (2007). On Non-Functional Requirements, 15th *IEEE International Requirements Engineering Conference (RE 2007)*, Delhi, India, (pp.21-26).

[Got95] Gotel, O. (1995). Contribution Structures for Requirements Traceability, London, England: Imperial College, Department of Computing.

[Gra92] Grady, R. B. (1992). *Practical Software Metrics for Project Management and Process Improvement*, NJ: Prentice-Hall.

[Gru93] Gruber, T. R. (1993). A Translation Approach to Portable Ontology Specifications, *Knowledge Acquisition Archive*, 5(2), (pp. 199- 220).

[HC88] Hauser, J. R., & Clausing, D. (1988). The House of Quality, *Harvard Business Review*, May – June 1988, (pp. 63- 73).

[HJ02] Holsapple, C.W. & Joshi, K.D. (2002). A Collaborative Approach to Ontology Design, *Communication of the ACM*, 45(2), (p.p. 42 - 47).

[HM06] Haruhiko, K. & Motoshi, S. (2006). Using domain ontology as domain knowledge for requirements elicitation, *proceedings of the 14th IEEE International Requirements Engineering Conference*, Minneapolis, USA, (pp. 186- 195).

[HNS05] Hofmeister, C., Nord, R.L., & Soni, D. (2005). Global Analysis: moving from software requirements specification to structural views of the software architecture, *IEEE Proceedings Software*, 152(4), (pp.187- 197).

[HS06] Happel, H., & Seedorf, S. (2006). Applications of Ontologies in Software Engineering, *In Proceeding of the Int'l Workshop on Semantic Web Enabled Software Engineering*.

[IBM] IBM website: SAS Hub Non Functional Requirements (NFRs): http://www.haifa.ibm.com/projects/software/nfr/index.html.

[IEEE6101290] Standard Glossary of Software Engineering Terminology. (1990). *IEEE Standard 610.12-1990*.

[IEEE83098] IEEE Std. 830-1998. (1998). IEEE recommended practice for software requirements specifications, *IEEE Transactions on Software Engineering*.

[IFPUG] FP Users Group: www.ifpug.org

[IFPUG99] IFPUG. (1999). *IFPUG Counting Practices Manual - Release. 4.1*, International Function Point Users Group, Westerville, OH.

[In98] In, H. (1998). *Conflict Identification and Resolution for Software Attribute Requirements*, Ph.D. Dissertation, USC, CA.

[ISO1414398] ISO 14143-1. (1998). International Standard ISO/IEC 14143-1, Information Technology – Software Measurement – Functional Size Measurement Part 1: Definition of Concepts.

[ISO1593907] International Standard ISO/IEC 15939 Second edition. (2007). Systems and software engineering —Measurement process.

[ISO1976103] ISO/IEC 19761. (2003). Software Engineering: COSMIC-FFP - A functional size measurement method, International Organization for Standardization – ISO, Geneva.

[ISO2092603] ISO 20926. (2003). *ISO/IEC 20926: Software Engineering - IFPUG 4.1 Unadjusted FSM Method -Counting Practices Manual*.

[ISO2096802] ISO 20968. (2002). *ISO/IEC 20968: Software Engineering - MkII Function Point Analysis – Counting Practices Manual*.

[ISO2457005] ISO 24570. (2005). *ISO/IEC 24570: Software Engineering - NESMA Functional Size Measurement Method v.2.1 - Definitions and Counting Guidelines for the Application of Function Point Analysis.*

[ISO25000] International Standard ISO/IEC 25000 Second edition. (2005). Software Engineering -- Software product Quality Requirements and Evaluation (SQuaRE) -- Guide to SQuaRE.

[ISO912601] International Standard ISO/IEC 9126-1. (2001). Software engineering – Product quality – Part 1: Quality model. ISO/IEC 9126-1:2001, 200.

[Jac07] Jacobs, D. (2007). Requirements Engineering so Things Don't Get Ugly, *Companion to the Proceeding of 29th International Conference on Software Engineering*, (pp. 159- 160).

[JBR99] Jacobson, I., Booch, G., & Rumbaugh, J. (1999). *The Unified Software Development Process*, Reading, Mass: Addison Wesley.

[Jin00] Jin, Z. (2000). Ontology-based requirements elicitation automatically, *Chinese Journal Computers,* 23(5), (pp. 486 – 492).

[JKCW08] Jingbai, T., Keqing, H., Chong, W., & Wei, L. (2008). A Context Awareness Non-functional Requirements Metamodel Based on Domain Ontology, *IEEE International Workshop on Semantic Computing and Systems*, Huangshan, China, (pp.1- 7).

[JM01] Juristo, N., & Moreno, A.M. (2001). *Basics of Software Engineering Experimentation, Kluwer.*

[Jon87] Jones, T. C. (1987). *A Short History of Function Points and Feature Points*, Software Productivity Research Inc., USA.

[Jur02] Jurjens, J. (2002). UMLsec: Extending UML for Secure Systems Development, *In UML '02: Proceedings of the 5th International Conference on The Unified Modeling Language*, London, UK, (pp. 412–425).

[Kam00] Kammelar, J. (2000). A sizing approach for OO-environments, *In Proceedings of the 4th International ECOOP Workshop on Quantitative Approaches in Object-Oriented Software Engineering.*

[Kar93] Karner, G. (1993*). Resource Estimation for Objectory Projects*, Objective Systems SF AB.

[Kas06] Kassab, M. (2006). *Towards an aspect-oriented software development model with quality measurements,* Thesis (M.Comp.Sc.)-Concordia University, Montreal, Canada.

[KBT07] Kiefer, C., Bernstein, A., & Tappolet, J. (2007). Analyzing Software with iSPARQL. *In Proceeding the 3rd ESWC International Workshop on Semantic Web Enabled Software Engineering.*

[KCO05] Kassab, M., Constantinides, C., & Ormandjieva, O. (2005). Specifying and Separating Concerns From Requirements to Design: a Case Study, *In The IASTED International Conference on Software Engineering (ACIT-SE 2005)*, Novosibirsk, Russia, (pp. 18–27).

[KDO07a] Kassab, M., Daneva, M., & Ormandjieva. O. (2007). Scope Management of the Non-Functional Requirements, *Proceedings of the 33rd Euromicro Conference on Software Engineering and Advanced Applications (SEAA)*, Lübeck, Germany, (pp. 409- 417).

[KDO07b] Kassab, M., Daneva, M., & Ormandjieva, O. (2007). Early Quantitative Assessment of Non-Functional Requirements, *Technical Report TR-CTIT-07-35 Centre for Telematics and Information Technology, University of Twente*, Enschede. ISSN 1381-3625.

[KDO09] Kassab, M., Daneva, M., & Ormandjieva, O. (2009). Towards an Early Software Effort Estimation based on Functional and Non-Functional Requirements, *Accepted at International Conference on Software Measurement, Software Process and Product Measurement*, Amsterdam, Netherlands.

[KICO5] Kazman, R., In, H. P. & Chen, H.-M. (2005). From Requirements Negotiation to Software Architecture Decisions, *Journal of Information and Software Technology*, 47 (9), (pp. 511-520).

[KK97] Kauffman, R., & Kumar, R. (1997). Investigating object-based metrics for representing software output size, *In Proceedings of the Conference on Information Systems and Technology (CIST)*, In the INFORMS 1997 Annual Conference, San Diego.

[KKK+06] Kappel, G., Kapsammer, E., Kargl, H., Kramler, G., Reiter, T., Retschitzegger, W., Schwinger, W., & Wimmer, M. (2006). Lifting Metamodels to Ontologies: A Step to the Semantic Integration of Modeling Languages. *In Proceeding of the ACM/IEEE 9th International Conference on Model Driven Engineering Languages and System*, (pp. 528–542).

[KKP90] Keller, S.E., Kahn, L.G., & Panara, R.B. (1990). Specifying Software Quality Requirements with Metrics. *In Thayer, R.H.; Dorfman. M.: System and Software Requirements Engineering, IEEE Computer Society Press*, Washington, (pp. 145- 163).

[Knu04] Knublauch, H. (2004). Ontology-Driven Software Development in the Context of the Semantic Web: An Example Scenario with Protege/OWL, *In Proceeding of 1st International Workshop on the Model-Driven Semantic Web*.

[KO06] Kassab, M., & Ormandjieva, O. (2006). Towards an Aspect-Oriented Software Development Model with Traceability Mechanism, *In Proceedings of the Early Aspects 2006: Traceability of Aspects in the Early Life Cycle Workshop*, Bonn, Germany.

[KOC05] Kassab, M., Ormandjieva, O., Constantinides, C. (2005). Providing Quality Measurement for Aspect-Oriented Software Development. *Proceedings of the 12th Asia-Pacific Software Engineering Conference*, Taipei, Taiwan, (pp. 769-7 75).

[KOD07a] Kassab, M., Ormandjieva, O., Daneva, M., & Abran. A. (2007). A. Non-Functional Requirements: Size Measurement and Testing with COSMIC-FFP, *Proceedings of the*

International Conference on Software Process and Product Measurement (IWSM-MENSURA 2007), Palma de Mallorca, Spain.

[KOD07b] Kassab, M., Ormandjieva, O., & Daneva. M. (2007). Towards a Scope Management of Non-Functional Requirements in Requirements Engineering, *Proceedings of the MeRePO7: Workshop on Measuring Requirements for Project and Product Success*, Palma de Mallorca, Spain.

[KOD08a] Kassab, M., Ormandjieva, & O., Daneva, M. (2008). A Traceability Metamodel for Change Management of Non-Functional Requirements, *Proceedings of the 6th international conference on Software Engineering Research, Management and Applications*, Prague, Czech Republic, (pp. 245- 254).

[KOD08b] Kassab, M., Ormandjieva, O., Daneva, M., & Abran, A. (2008). A Non-Functional Requirements Size Measurement Method (NFSM) with COSMIC-FFP, *Lecture Notes in Computer Science (LNCS) 4895 – 0168*, Springer–Verlag Beriln Heidelberg, (pp. 168-182).

[KOD08c] Kassab, M., Ormandjieva, O., & Daneva, M. (2008). A Meta-model for the Assessment of Non-Functional Requirements Size, *Proceedings of the 34th EuroMicro SEAA Conference*. 2008, Parma, Italy, (pp. 411-418).

[KOD09a] Kassab, M., Ormandjieva, O., & Daneva, M. (2009). A Metamodel for Tracing Non-Functional Requirements, *Proceedings of the 2009 World Congress on Computer Science and Information Engineering (CSIE 2009)*, Los Angeles, USA.

[KOD09b] Kassab, M., Ormandjieva, O., & Daneva, M. (2009). An Ontology Based Approach to Non-Functional Requirements Conceptualization, *Accepted at the the Fourth International Conference on Software Engineering Advances, ICSEA 2009*, Porto, Portugal.

[KOD10] Kassab, M., Ormandjieva, O., & Daneva, M. (2010). Managing the Changes and the Attainable Scope of Non-Functional Requirements in Software Engineering, *Accepted as a book chapter to Methodologies for Non-Functional Requirements in Service Oriented Architecture*.

[KS05] Kaiya, H., & Saeki, M. (2005). Ontology based requirements analysis: lightweight semantic processing approach, *proceedings of the 5th International Conference on Quality Software (QSIC)*, Melbourne, Australia, (pp. 223 – 230).

[KS98] Kotonya, G., & Sommerville, I. (1998). *Requirements Engineering: Processes and Techniques*, John Wiley & Sons.

[KU95] King, M., & Uschold, M. (1995). Towards a Methodology for Building Ontologies, *Workshop on Basic Ontological Issues in Knowledge Sharing IJCAI*, Montreal, Canada, (pp. 6.1-6.10).

[LBD02] Lodderstedt, T., Basin, D. A., & Doser, J. (2002). SecureUML: A UMLBased Modeling Language for Model-Driven Security, *In UML '02: Proceedings of the 5th International Conference on The Unified Modeling Language*, London, UK, (pp. 426- 441).

[LDS05] Lock, R., Dobson, G., & Sommerville, I. (2005). Quality of Service Requirement Specification using an Ontology, Conference *Proceedings 1st International Workshop on*

Service-Oriented Computing: Consequences for Engineering Requirements (SOCCER'05), Paris, France.

[Lee96] Lee, M. (1996). *Foundation of the WinWin Requirements Negotiation System*, Ph.D. Dissertation, USC, CA.

[Let02] Letelier, P. (2002). A Framework for Requirements Traceability in UML-Based Projects, *Proceeding of the 1st International Workshop on Traceability in Emerging Forms of Software Engineering*, Edinburgh, (pp. 30−41).

[LG05] Lee, S.W., & Gandhi, R.A. (2005). Ontology-based Active Requirements Engineering Framework, *In Proceeding of the 12th Asia-Pacific Software Engineering Conference*, (pp. 481-490).

[LMGYA06] Lee, S. W., Muthurajan, D., Gandhi, R.A., Yavagal, D., & Ahn, G. (2006). Building Decision Support Problem Domain Ontology From Natural Language Requirements for Software Assurance, *International Journal of Software Engineering and Knowledge Engineering*, 16(6), (pp. 851-884).

[LS05] Liebchen, G. A., & Shepperd, M. (2005). Software Productivity Analysis of a Large Data Set and Issues of Confidentiality and Data Quality, *In Proceedings of the 11th IEEE international Software Metrics Symposium* (September 19 - 22, 2005), METRICS, IEEE Computer Society, Washington, DC, 46.

[LT93] Leveson, L., & Turner, C. S. (1993). An Investigation of the Therac-25 Accidents, *IEEE Computer*, 26(7), (pp. 18-41).

[LW03] Leffingwell D., & Widrig, D. (2003). *Managing Software Requirements: A Unified Approach*, The Addison-Wesley Object Technology Series.

[LWHS01] Lokan, C., Wright, T., Hill, P. R., & Stringer, M. (2001). Organizational Benchmarking Using the ISBSG Data Repository, *IEEE Software*, 18(5), (pp. 26-32).

[Lyu96] Lyu, M.R. (1996). *Handbook of Software Reliability Engineering*, McGraw-Hill.

[MA04] Mendes, O., & Abran, A. (2004). Software Engineering Ontology: A Development Methodology, 9, *Metrics News*, (pp. 68-76).

[MAB02] Moreira, A., Araujo, J., & Brito I. (2002). Crosscutting Quality Attributes for Requirements Engineering, *In 14th International Conference on Software Engineering and Knowledge Engineering* 2002, Ischia, Italy, (pp. 167-174).

[MAHO00] Meli, R., Abran, A., Ho, V. T., & Oligny, S. (2000). On the Applicability of COSMIC-FFP for Measuring Software Throughout its Life Cycle, *In Proceedings of the Escom-Scope*.

[Max09] Maxwell, K. (2009). The PROMISE Repository of Software Engineering Databases, School of Information Technology and Engineering, University of Ottawa, Canada, Available: http://promise.site.uottawa.ca/SERepository.

[MBM94] Matson, J. E., Barret, B. E., & Mellichamp, J. M. (1994). Software development cost estimation using Function Points, *IEEE Transactions Software Engineering, 20*(4), (pp. 275–287).

[MRW77] McCall, J., Richards, P., Walters, G. (1977). Factors in Software Quality, NTIS.

[Mcc06] McConnell, S. (2006). *Software Estimation: Demystifying the Black Art,* Microsoft Press.

[MCN92] Mylopoulos, J., Chung, L., & Nixon, B. (1992). Representing and Using Nonfunctional Requirements: A process Oriented Approach, *IEEE Transactions in Software Engineering,* 18(6), (pp. 483-497).

[Mel97a] Meli, R. (1997). Early and extended Function Point: A new method for Function Points estimation, *In Proceedings of the IFPUG-Fall Conference,* 15–19 September, Scottsdale, Arizona.

[Mel97b] Meli, R. (1997). Early Function Points: A new estimation method for software projects, *In Proceedings of ESCOM 97,* Berlin, Germany.

[MERCEDES97] Mercedes A-Class: Mercedes: Wie sicher ist die AKlasse?. (1997). *German news magazine: Der Spiegel,* ISSN 0038- 7452, October 27, 1997, (p.p. 120); English translation: http://www.geocities.com/MotorCity/downs/9323/aclacap.htm, last visited on February 11, 2005.

[MF00] Maxwell, K. D., & Forselius, P. (2000). Benchmarking Software-Development Productivity, *IEEE Software,* 17(1), (pp. 80-88).

[MKII98] MKII. (1998). *The United Kingdom Software Metrics Association: MkII Function Point Analysis Counting Practices Manual v. 1.3.1*

[MP08] Magazinovic, A., & Pernstål, J. (2008). Any other cost estimation inhibitors?, *In Proceedings of the Second ACM-IEEE international Symposium on Empirical Software Engineering and Measurement,* Kaiserslautern, Germany, ESEM '08. ACM, New York, NY, (pp. 233-242).

[MRG+04] Mousavi, M., Rusello, G., Ghaudron, M., Reniers, M., Basten, T., Corsaro, A., Shukla, S., Gupta, R., & Schmidt, D. (2004). ASpects + GAMMA = AspectGAMMA: A Formal Framework for ASpect-Oriented Specification, *In Workshop on Aspect-Oriented Modeling with UML in Conjunction with 1st International Conference on Aspect-Oriented Software Development,* Enshede, Netherlands.

[Myl06] Mylopoulos, J., (2006). Goal-oriented Requirements Engineering, *Keynote speech at the 14th IEEE International Conference on Requirements Engineering, IEEE Computer Society Press.*

[NAB04] Nagy, I., Aksit, M., & Bergmans, L. (2004). Composition Graphs: A Foundation for Reasoning About Aspect-Oriented Composition, In 5th Aspect-Oriented Modeling Workshop in Conjunction with UML 2004, Lisbon, Portugal.

[NCI03]   National   Cancer   Institute   (NCI)   Thesaurus.   (2003). http://www.mindswap.org/2003/CancerOntology/

[Ncu00] Ncube, C. (2000). *A Requirements Engineering Method for COTS-Based Systems Development*, Ph.D. Thesis, City University London.

[NESMA97] NESMA. (1997). *Definitions and Counting Guidelines for the Application of Function Point Analysis*, v.2.0.

[NI07] Niemelä, E., & Immonen, A. (2007). Capturing Quality Requirements of Product Family Architecture, *Information and Software Technology*, 49(11- 12), (pp. 1107-1120).

[NLC00] Neto, D., Leite, J., Cysneiros, L. (2000). Non-Functional Requirements for Object-Oriented Modeling. *In third Workshop on Requirements Engineering*, Rio de Janeiro, Brazil, (pp.109–125).

[NM00] Noy, N., & Mc Guinness, D. (2000). Ontology Development 101: A Guide to Creating Your First Ontology, *Technical Report KSL-01-05*, Stanford University.

[OKC05] Ormandjieva, O., Kassab, M., Constantinides, C. (2005). Measurement of Cohesion and Coupling in OO Analysis Model Based on Crosscutting Concerns. *Proceedings of the International Workshop on Software Measurements*, Montreal, Quebec, Canada.

[OWL] W3C, Web Ontology Language (OWL), http://www.w3.org/2004/OWL.

[PAMT01] Pastor, O., Abrahao, S. M., Molina, J. C., & Torres, I. (2001). A FPA-like measure for object oriented systems from conceptual models, *In Proceedings of the 11th International Workshop on Software Measurement* (IWSM'01), Montreal, Canada, Shaker Verlag, (pp. 51–69).

[Par92] Park, R. (1992). Software Size Measurement: A Framework for Counting Source Lines of Code, *Software Engineering Institute Technical Report*.

[PDKV02] Paech, B., Dutoit, A., Kerkow, D., & Von Knethen, A. (2002). Functional requirements, non-functional requirements and architecture specification cannot be separated - *A position paper, 8th International Workshop on Requirements Engineering: Foundation for Software Quality*, Essen, Germany.

[PKL04] Park, D., Kang, S., & Lee, J. (2004). Design Phase Analysis of Software Performance Using Aspect Oriented Programming, *In 5th Aspect-Oriented Modeling Workshop in Conjunction with UML 2004*, Lisbon, Portugal.

[PMBOK00] PMBOK. (2000). Project Management Body of Knowledge Guide 2000. See http://www.pmi.org/info/PP_PMBOKGuide2000Excerpts.pdf

[Pre97] Pressman, R.S. (1997). *Software Engineering A Practitioner's Approach*, McGraw-Hill.

[PROTÉGÉ] Protégé, http://protege.stanford.edu/

[PWL05] Pfleeger, S. L., Wu, F., & Lewis, R. (2005). *Software Cost Estimation and Sizing Methods: Issues and Guidelines,* RAND Corporation.

[RACER] Racer: Renamed Abox and Concept Expression Reasoner. http://www.sts.tu-harburg.de/~r.f.moeller/racer/

[RCJo2] Rosa, N. S., Cunha, P. R. F., & Justo, G. R. R. (2002). Process NFL: A language for Describing Non-Functional Properties, Proceeding 35th HICSS, IEEE Press, (pp.3676-3685).

[Rei90] Reifer, D. J. (1990). Asset-R: A function point sizing tool for scientific and real-time systems, *Journal System Software, 11* (3), (pp. 159–171).

[RJo1] Ramesh, B., & Jarke, M. (2001). Toward a Reference Model for Requirements Traceability, *IEEE Transactions on Software Engineering,* 27(1), (pp. 58-93).

[RMA03] Rashid, A., Moreira A., & Araujo, J. (2003). Modularisation and Composition of Aspectual Requirements, *In 2nd International Conference on Aspect-Oriented,* Boston, MA, (pp. 11–20).

[RR99] Robertson, S., & Robertson, J. (1999). *Mastering the Requirements Process,* Addison-Wesley Professional.

[RSMA02] Rashid, A., Sawyer, P., Moreira, A., & Araujo. J. (2002). Early Aspects: A model for Aspect Oriented Requirements Engineering, *In IEEE Joint International Conference on Requirements Engineering,* IEEE Computer Press, (pp. 199–202).

[Samo6] Salem, A. M. (2006). Improving Software Quality through Requirements Traceability Models, *Proceedings of International Conference on Computer Systems and Applications,* (pp. 1159- 1162).

[SBMB06] Sack, P. M. O. O., Bouneffa, M., Maweed, Y., & Basson, H. (2006). On Building an Integrated and Generic Platform for Software Quality Evaluation, *2nd IEEE International Conference on Information and Communication technologies: From Theory to Applications,* Umayyad Palace, Damascus, Syria, (pp. 2872-2877).

[SC04] Supakkul, S., & Chung, L. (2004*).* Integrating FRs and NFRs: A use case and goal driven approach, *In Proceedings of the 2nd International Conference on Software Engineering Research, Management and Applications (SERA),* Los Angeles, CA, (pp. 30-37).

[SC05] Sicilia, M.A., & Chadrado-Gallego, J.J. (2005). Linking Software Engineering concepts to upper ontologies, *Proceedings of the First Workshop on Ontology, Conceptualizations and Epistemology for Software and Systems Engineering,* Alcalá de Henares, Spain.

[SCREEN99] SCREEN. (1999). *Glossary of EU SCREEN Project.* http://cordis.europa.eu/infowin/acts/rus/projects/screen/ glossary/glossary.htm (visited 2007-07 05)

[SDM05] Seffah, A., Desmarais, M., & Metzger, M. (2005). *Human-Centered Software Engineering,* Springer.

[SIEMENS04] Siemens Warns of Possible Hearing Damage in Some Cell Phones. (2004). http://www.consumeraffairs.com/news04/siemens_mobile.html, last visited on Aug, 4th, 2009.

[Sim81] Simon, H. (1981). *The sciences of the Artificial, Second Edition.* Cambridge, MA: The MIT Press.

[Sku02] Skulmoski, G. (2002). Shifting Gears: the De Facto Global Standard for Project Management. See http://www.pmi-lakeshore.org/present_20020311_Shifting_Gears.ppt

[SOKH09] Shaban-Nejad, A., Ormandjieva, O., Kassab, M., & Haarslev, V. (2009). Managing Requirement Volatility in an Ontology-Driven Clinical Laboratory Information Management System (LIMS) Using Category Theory, *The International Journal of Telemedicine and Applications*, Volume 2009.

[STANDISH09] Standish Group. (2009). *The CHAOS Report*, April 23, 2009, Boston.

[Ste01] Stensrud, E. (2001). Alternative Approaches to Effort Prediction of ERP projects, *Journal of Information and Software Technology*, 43 (7), (pp. 413-423).

[STW03] Shanks, G., Tansley, E., & Weber, R. (2003). Using Ontology to Validate Conceptual Models, *Communication of the ACM*, 46(10), (p.p. 85 – 98).

[SURVEY1] A Survey of Non-Functional Requirements in Software Development Process: http://lacl.univ-paris12.fr/Rapports/TR/TR-LACL-2008-7.pdf

[SWRL]: SWRL: A Semantic Web Rule Language Combining OWL and RuleML, http://www.w3.org/Submission/SWRL/

[Sym88] Symons, C. (1988). Function Point analysis: Difficulties and improvements, *IEEE Transactions Software Engineering, 14(1)*, (pp. 2–11).

[TA05] Tyree, J., & Akerman, A. (2005). Architecture Decisions: Demystifying Architecture, *IEEE Software*, 22(2), (pp.19-27).

[TBB04] Tessier, F., Badri, L., & Badri, M. (2004). Towards a Formal Detection of Semantic Conflicts Between Aspects: A Model Based Approach. *In 5th ASpect-Oriented Modeling Workshop in Conjunction with UML 2004*, Lisbon, Portugal.

[TD90] Thayer, R.H., & Dorfman, M. (1990). Standards, Guidelines and Examples on System and Software Requirements Engineering, IEEE *Computer Society (New York)*.

[TEMPLATE09] Scenario Plus, Qualities and Constraints, or Non Functional Requirements Template. (2009). http://www.scenarioplus.org.uk/download_nfrs.html

[Teo99] Teologlou, G. (1999). *Measuring OO Software with Predictive Object Points*, Shaker Publications, ISBN 90-423-0075-2.

[UKSMA02] UKSMA. (2002). Estimating with Mark II,v.1.3.1., ISO/IEC 20968:2002(E), www.uksma.co.uk

[UW02] Ullman, J., & Widom, J. (2002). *Database Systems: The Complete Book*, Prentice Hall.

[WADD03] Wille, C., Abran, A., Desharnais, J.M., & Dumke, R.R. (2003). The quality concepts and subconcepts in SWEBOK: An ontology challenge, *In proceeding Of the 2003 International Workshop on Software Measurement (IWSM)*, (pp. 113-130).

[Whi92] Whitmire, S. (1992). 3D Function Points: Scientific and real-time extensions to Function Points, *In Proceedings of the Pacific Northwest Software Quality Conference*.

[Whi97] Whitmire, S. (1997). *Object Oriented Design Measurement*, John Wiley & Sons.

[Wie00] Wieringa, R. (2000). The Declarative Problem Frame: Designing Systems that Create and Use Norms, *Proceeding Of the 10th IEEE International Workshop on Software Specification and Design*, IEEE Computer Society Press, (pp. 75-85).

[Wie03] Wiegers, K. (2003). *Software Requirements*, 2nd edition, Microsoft Press.

[WIKIPEDIA-NFR] Wikipedia: *Non-Functional Requirements:* http://en.wikipedia.org/wiki/Non-functional_requirements (visited 2007-07-05).

[WIKIPEDIA-RA] Wikipedia: *Requirements Analysis:* http://en.wikipedia.org /wiki/Requirements_analysis (visited 2007-07-05)

[WRHRW00] Wohlin, C., Runeson, P., Höst, M., Regnell, B., & Wesslén, A. (2000). *Experimentation in Software Engineering*, Springer.

[WSZA06] Winter, V., Siy, H., Zand, M., & Aryal, P. (2006). Early Aspects Workshop at AOSD'06, Bonn, Germany.

[WW03] Weber, M., & Wesbrot, J. (2003). Requirements Engineering in Automotive Development: Experiences and Challenges, *IEEE Software,* 20(1), (pp.16-24).

[WZR07] Witte, R., Zhang, Y., & Rilling, J., (2007). Empowering Software Maintainers with Semantic Web Technologies, *In Proceeding of the 4th European Semantic Web Conference*, Springer, (pp. 37–52).

[XQUERY] W3C XML Query (XQuery): http://www.w3.org/XML/Query/

[XZRL05] Xu, L., Ziv, H., Richardson, D., & Liu, Z. (2005). Towards modeling nonfunctional requirements in software architecture, *In Proceedings of Aspect-Oriented Software Design, Workshop on Aspect-Oriented Requirements Engineering and Architecture Design*, Chicago, Illinois.

[YHLWB08] Yang, Y., He, M., Li, M., Wang, Q., & Boehm, B. (2008). Phase distribution of software development effort, In *Proceedings of the Second ACM-IEEE international Symposium on Empirical Software Engineering and Measurement* (Kaiserslautern, Germany, October 09 - 10, 2008), ESEM '08, ACM, New York, NY, (pp. 61-69).

[ZG07] Zhu, L., & Gorton, I., (2007). UML Profiles for Design Decisions and Non-Functional Requirements, *In 2nd International Workshop on SHAring and Reusing architectural Knowledge Rational and Design Intent*, (pp. 8- 15).

Appendix A:

Table A-1: Quality Requirements Hierarchy.

#	Quality	Definition	Parent Quality
1	Accessibility	The degree to which a product is accessible by as many people as possible.	Testability [BBL76]. Efficiency [BBL76]. Utility [Fir03]. Usability [RR99].
2	Accountability	Obligation imposed by law, or lawful order, or regulation, on an entity for storage of accurate property data.	Testability [BBL76]. Efficiency [BBL76].
3	Accuracy	The capability of the software product to provide the right or agreed results or effects with the needed degree of precision.	Functionality quality [ISO912601]. Integrity [CNYM00]. Reliability [BBL76]. Correctness [Fir03].
4	Adaptability	The ease with which conformance to standards can be checked.	Portability [ISO912601].
5	Analyzability	The quality that characterizes the ability to identify the root cause of a failure within the software.	Maintainability [ISO912601].
6	Attractiveness	The capability of the software product to be attractive to the user.	Usability [BTV06].
7	Augmentability	Quality that indicates the ability to make the software greater, as in size or quantity.	Structuredness [BBL76].
8	Availability	Quality that refers to the frequency of system outages that lead to unavailability of the system usage by the users.	Security [CNYM00]. Dependability [Fir03].

9	BootStartTime	The time for executing the operations required for restarting up the software.	Time behavior [TEMPLATE09].
10	Capacity	The maximum production possible. (e.g.: the amount of information (in bytes) that can be stored on a disk drive.	Behavior quality [TEMPLATE09].
11	Changeability	The quality that characterizes the amount of effort to change a system.	Maintainability [ISO912601].
12	Co-existence	The ability of an application to share an environment with other applications without experiencing or causing negative effects.	Portability [ISO912601].
13	Communicativeness	The trait of being communicative.	Testability [BBL76].
14	Completeness	The degree to which full implementation of required function has been achieved.	Integrity [CNYM00]. Reliability [BBL76].
15	Compliance	The degree to which the software is complied with certain specifications and guidelines.	Functionality quality requirement [ISO912601].
16	Conciseness	The degree to which a software system or component has no excessive information present.	Understandability [BBL76].
17	Confidentiality	The quality that refers to the access to the data. Only authorized persons can get an access to the data in a system.	Security [CNYM00].
18	Configurability	In Communications or computer systems, a configuration is an arrangement of functional units according to their nature, number, and chief.	Utility [Fir03].
19	Consistency	The use of uniform design and documentation techniques throughout the	Accuracy [CNYM00]. Reliability [BBL76].

		software development project.	Understandability [BBL76].
20	Correct-ability	A developer-oriented quality requirement specifying the part of maintainability that measures the ease with which defects shall be able to be fixed.	Maintainability [RR99].
21	Correctness	The degree to which software performs its desired function.	Quality requirement [Firo3].
22	Currency	The property of belonging to the present time.	Correctness [Firo3].
23	Dependability	The ability to deliver service that can justifiably be trusted by users.	Quality requirement [Firo3].
24	Device Efficiency	The degree to which the device is efficient.	Efficiency quality [BBL76].
25	DeviceIndependence	The process of making the software accessible by any device under any circumstance and by all people.	Portability [BBL76].
26	Effectiveness	The degree to which program or system objectives are being achieved.	Quality in use [ISO912601].
27	Efficiency	The amount of computing resources and code required by a program to perform its function.	External and internal quality characteristic [ISO912601].
28	Environmental Tolerance	The ability of a system to work in a variety of conditions and locales.	Robustness [Firo3].
29	Error Tolerance	The ability of a system or component to continue normal operation despite the presence of erroneous inputs.	Robustness [Firo3].
30	Extensibility	System design principle where the implementation takes into consideration future growth.	Maintainability [RR99].
31	External	This is a special case of Confidentiality with	Confidentiality

		focus on the external aspect of the product.	[CNYM00].
32	External Consistency	This is a special case of Consistency with focus on the external aspect of the product.	Consistency [CNYM00].
33	Failure Tolerance	This is a special case of Fault tolerance in which the error cause the system to fail.	Robustness [Firo3].
34	FaultTolerance	The property that enables a system to continue operating properly in the event of the failure of (or one or more faults within) some of its components.	Reliability [ISO912601].
35	Functionality	A set of attributes that bear on the existence of a set of functions and their specified properties.	External and internal quality [ISO912601].
36	Installability	The quality that Characterizes the effort required to install the software.	Portability [ISO912601]. Utility [Firo3].
37	Integrity	The ability of a system to withstand attacks to its security.	Security [CNYM00]. Reliability [BBL76].
38	Internal Confidentiality	This is a special case of Confidentiality with focus on the internal aspect of the product.	Confidentiality [CNYM00].
39	Internal Consistency	This is a special case of Consistency with focus on the internal aspect of the product.	Consistency [CNYM00].
40	Internationalization	Internationalization and localization are means of adapting computer software to different languages and regional differences.	Utility [Firo3].
41	Interoperability	The ability of two or more systems or components to exchange information and to use the information that has been exchanged.	Functionality quality requirement [ISO912601].
42	Learnability	The capability of a software product to enable the user to learn how to use it.	Usability [ISO912601] and [RR99]
43	Legibility	The quality of being readable or	Understandability

		distinguishable by the eye.	[TEMPLATE09].
44	Main Memory	The quality that describes the amount of usage of Main Memory by the software.	Space quality [CNYM00].
45	Maintainability	The ability to change the system to deal with new technology or to fix defects.	External and internal quality [ISO912601].
46	Maturity	This quality characteristic concerns frequency of failure of the software.	Reliability [ISO912601].
47	OneToOneAccuracy	This is a special case of Accuracy.	Accuracy [CNYM00].
48	Operability	The ease of operation of a program.	Usability [ISO912601]. Utility [Fir03].
49	Performance	The responsiveness of the system—the time required to respond to stimuli (events) or the number of events processed in some interval of time.	Efficiency [TEMPLATE09].
50	Personalization	The quality refers to the ability of the software to be adapted to the needs of an individual.	Utility [Fir03].
51	Portability	The ability of the system to run under different computing environments.	External and internal quality [ISO912601].
52	Precision	Precision of a numerical quantity is a measure of the detail in which the quantity is expressed.	Correctness [Fir03].
53	Productivity	The unit of product produced per unit of input.	Quality in use [ISO912601].
54	PropertyAccuracy	This is a special case of Accuracy.	Accuracy [CNYM00].
55	Recoverability	Ability to bring back a failed system to full operation, including data and network connections.	Reliability [ISO912601].
56	Reliability	The ability of a system or component to perform its required functions under stated conditions for a specified period of time.	External and internal quality [ISO912601]. Dependability

			[Firo3].
57	Replaceability	The capability of the software product to be used in place of another specified software product for the same purpose in the same environment.	Portability [ISO912601].
58	ResourceBehavior	The quality which characterizes resources used, i.e. memory, CPU, disk and network usage.	Efficiency behavior [ISO912601].
59	ResponseTime	Reaction time: the time that elapses between a stimulus and the response to it.	Time behavior [TEMPLATE09] and [CNYM00].
60	Robustness	The degree to which a system or component can function correctly in the presence of invalid inputs or stressful environmental conditions.	Dependability [Firo3].
61	Safety	No consensus in the system's engineering about what is meant by the term "safety requirements". The informal definition: safety requirements are the "shall not" requirements which exclude situations from the possible solution of the system.	Quality in use [ISO912601].
62	Satisfaction	Act of fulfilling a desire or need or appetite; "the satisfaction of their demand for better services.	Quality in use [ISO912601].
63	Schedualability	Refers to the way processes are assigned to run on the available resources. This assignment is carried out by software known as a scheduler.	Performance [Firo3].
64	Secondary Storage	The quality describes the amount of usage of secondary storage by the software or component.	Space [CNYM00].
65	Security	A measure of the system's ability to resist unauthorized attempts at usage and denial	Functionality quality [ISO912601].

		of service while still providing its services to legitimate users.	Dependability quality [Firo3].
66	SelfContainedness	The degree to which the source code provides meaningful documentation.	Reliability [BBL76]. Portability [BBL76].
67	SelfDescriptivness	An adjective meaning "It describes itself".	Testability [BBL76].
68	Space	The quality describes the amount of usage of space by the software or component.	Efficiency [TEMPLATE09]. Performance [CNYM00].
69	Stability	The quality that characterizes the sensitivity to change of a given system that is the negative impact that may be caused by system changes.	Maintainability [ISO912601].
70	Structuredness	The degree to which a system or component possesses a definite pattern of organization of its interdependent parts	Changeability [BBL76]. Understandability [BBL76].
71	Subset-ability	The ability to support the production of a subset of the system.	Utility [Firo3].
72	Suitability	The appropriateness (to specification) of the functions of the software.	Functionality quality [ISO912601].
73	Survivability	The degree to which essential functions are still available even though some part of the system is down.	Dependability [Firo3].
74	Testability	The ability to discover faults by well-defined test cases.	Maintainability [ISO912601].
75	Throughput	Output relative to input; the amount passing through a system from input to output (especially of a computer program over a period of time).	Time behavior quality [TEMPLATE09].
76	Time Accuracy	This is a special case of Accuracy quality.	Accuracy to [CNYM00].

77	Time Behavior	The quality characterizes response times for a given throughput, i.e. transaction rate.	Efficiency [ISO912601]. Performance [CNYM00].
78	Transportability	The ability of software and courseware to be developed on one computer, and then used on another one.	Utility [Firo3].
79	Type and Position of Device	The quality related to type and position of device used as a resource for the software.	Resource behavior [TEMPLATE09].
80	Understandability	The ability to understand the software readily, in order to change/fix it.	Usability [ISO912601].
81	Usability	The ease with which a user can learn to operate, prepare inputs for, and interpret outputs of a system or component.	External and internal quality [ISO912601]. Utility [Firo3].
82	UsageTime	The time that is required for using the software functionality.	Time behavior [TEMPLATE09].
83	Value Accuracy	This is a special case of Accuracy.	Accuracy [CNYM00].
84	Variability	The quality that refers to how well the architecture can be expanded or modified to produce new architectures that differ in specific, preplanned ways.	Utility [Firo3].
85	Withdraw-ability	The quality that refers to the ability to discontinue the usage of the software. The degree of ability to remove from consideration or participation.	Utility [Firo3].
86	Work Load Distribution	The quality of distribution of the quantity of processing among available resources.	Resource behavior [TEMPLATE09].
87	Workload	The quantity of processing to include the machine cycles and the disk I/Os.	Time behavior [TEMPLATE09].